My Love Affair with Buffalo Billy

and the Beginning of
Buffalo Billy's Bison Brotherhood

by Billy's Auntie

My Love Affair with Buffalo Billy
Copyright © 2014 by Billy's Auntie

Cover by: Laura Rose McLeod

ISBN-13: 978-1497495142
ISBN-10: 1497495148
Library of Congress Control Number: [2014906178]

Book Website
www.myloveaffairwithbuffalobilly.com

Email: myloveaffairwithbuffalobilly@aol.com

Printed in U.S.A

Dedication

I have always called this Billy's Book and it is dedicated
to him and to all bison for all that they have endured
at the hands of nature and worse, by man. I hope Billy
and I can make a difference.

To my Mother, who has always been there, and to my
cousin Patty Anderson for her steadfast support. To my
friend Laura who gave of her time and her
talent so Billy's Book would be read, and to
Jack Hale who made sure of it.

But most of all,
I thank God for His BIGGEST gift of a lifetime
. . . . my Buffalo Billy.

Prologue

I never imagined that I would fall in love with an American Icon. Well, at least not one with a scruffy beard, hair everywhere, and as stocky as an SUV. I always had iconic aspirations, but I thought the object of my heart skipping a beat would be of the two-legged variety. I also never imagined that a buffalo could actually fall in love with me too. However, a buffalo named, Billy, changed my life in immeasurable ways and decidedly determined who I have become.

I have not thought of myself as a complicated person, but since I've never thought anyone has really understood me, maybe I am. But Billy "got me." He understood how I could actually love sloshing around in the muck so he would have a clean barn, while wearing designer perfume. He also thought it was perfectly normal that I'd choose to wear pink and green floral rubber boots while doing it.

Because of my love and devotion to a buffalo, my friends thought I had gone completely mad, or they thought perhaps my hormone level had caused some temporary insanity. But Billy understood that I had found my passion in him.

He accepted all that jabbering I did for hours on end, talking to him in one-way conversations. Then there were times when my blabbermouth closed tightly shut if it meant keeping quiet would protect him. My friends would roll their eyes while listening to my over-the-top loving conversations with Billy, but he and I coveted every sappy minute of it.

I would come home from a social event, toss off my party outfit, eager to change into stained and worn "buffalo clothes." Then I'd squash down my hair, the same hair that I had spent an hour fixing, and don a dusty straw hat that would cause my perspiration soaked bangs to stick flat to my forehead. It definitely wasn't a good look, but Billy loved that hat. A good manicure would only last me about four hours...until I dug my hands into a sack of sweet cob and tore apart bales of prickly alfalfa. I loved hand feeding that boy as much as he did. He didn't care about things like nail polish, and I didn't mind having hands slathered with buffalo slobber.

I am an interior designer by profession. I love and appreciate everything beautiful and fine. I am drawn to the best of the best in all things. I never tire of working with luscious silks and elegant furnishings. I spend hours admiring the smallest of details in everything beautiful that few people would even notice…beautiful places, beautiful things, and the pursuit of aesthetics in everything. But in my beautiful world, nothing is a lovely as nature, and nature's finest is the American Bison. Buffalo Billy was, judged in my heart, the epitome of buffalo perfection. I spent every day admiring that magnificent beast, and neither of us ever tired of it.

Growing up, my father saw no difference between having an only child be a girl or a boy. We tied our own flies together and went fishing. We shared the love of nature, camping in the back of a frigid, cramped, cargo van. We experienced the thrill of seeing all sorts of wildlife, who in turn thought we were a curiosity. We shared the thrill of catching trout, and then we felt the bigger rush of letting them go. We'd smell pretty ripe to others by the time we came home. But we never noticed, all bundled up close in our sleeping bags, laughing ourselves silly, sharing the same sense of humor.

On other occasions, I would get all dressed up in a pretty little dress, insisting upon matching hair ribbons and fancy socks, and my Dad and I would go to the movies and to dinner, holding hands wherever we went. The word "girly" was not used back then, but my Dad would not have liked the term. All things feminine he thoroughly encouraged and embraced with me.

So as an adult, it was natural for me to seek all the best things in life, both tangible and obscure, material and natural, and not be bound by convention in any form. Contradictions are what make my life full and rich, which can be perplexing to others. In this conventional world, I stand out like a white buffalo in a herd of solid brown. Billy understood all of that and thought I was perfect, for a human, just the way I am.

I am a sucker for the downtrodden, always ready to trust and help all sorts of varmints, both animal and human. It's always the human ones who will disappoint. I love Christianity for its perfect moral ideals, and am constantly frustrated that I come up so short of attaining them. It's the ultimate disappointment and challenge, but I keep on trying with terminal persistence.

I can be relentless and buffalo hide tough when faced with circumstances of right and wrong or injustice. I believe in the story of David and Goliath.

In grade school I remember slugging the school bully in the mouth during recess in front of a startled pint sized crowd, wearing my favorite lavender dress with the tulle fluffy slip. That party dress wasn't designed for schoolyard slugfests, and with that right punch it simultaneously ripped along the seam, and the slip flew up revealing my brown and lime green plaid (definitely not party) cotton underpants. I cried all the way home knowing my parents were right to advise me not to show off my dress at school and risk ruining it. . . . and now I was also burdened with a bruised reputation not only in behavior, but in lingerie selection. But ruining my dress and my ego didn't matter as much as showing off a mean right hook to a bully who hounded my retarded friend, especially when it meant that the bullying would stop. . . . at least in my presence. The value of a friend meant everything.

Ironically, my nemesis is confrontation, and I try everything to avoid it. Unfortunately, all too often it seems to enjoy finding and torturing me. Although I'd rather be subjected to a room full of giant, hairy tarantulas than be involved in a confrontation, once it's begun, it won't be me who backs down.

I have always been open to reveal who I am to others, but it was Billy who really defined me. He understood and happily accepted all of my idiosyncrasies and contradictions. After all, what was accepting a little eccentricity compared to receiving full-blown unconditional love and devotion...the kind that lasts forever.

This is our story. It was always all about him... my precious Buffalo Billy.

My Love Affair with Buffalo Billy

Change of Life

In the summer of 2007, I was a guest at my favorite place, the venerable Hotel Ritz in Paris. Staying at the Ritz is like being on vacation with a doting Sugar Daddy. The Hotel will wrap you in its luxurious arms and take complete care of you. Any wish you desire will be granted, as the word "no" does not exist at the Hotel Ritz.

From the hotel, I took a limousine on a Sunday side trip to my favorite home: Louis XIV's Versailles. The sun was not shining down on the Sun King's palace that day. Instead there was a soft rain with the most beautiful golden light casting down from the clouds. As I walked the paths of the beautiful gardens of the estate, everything appeared to be enveloped in this luxurious glow, trapped in a perfect, surreal vision. It seemed like a fantasy that might disappear if I paused to blink.

Most of the visitors were scrambling to avoid the rain, but I was sheltered by a signature blue Ritz umbrella, given to me protectively by the Hotel's concierge. I was wearing my favorite silk velvet coat with a matching scarf draped around my neck, stylishly shielding me from the chill. My blonde hair was tucked under a wide brimmed felt hat that perfectly matched my glossy red Chanel lipstick.

On Sundays during the summer, the Chateau plays glorious classical music through hidden outside speakers, as visitors stroll past gushing, baroque fountains and admire the various manicured park settings. I was walking the same path, admiring the same view, and even listening to the same music that Marie Antoinette enjoyed over 200 years ago. I too lost my head during that magical afternoon, feeling overwhelmingly happy, content, and completely in the moment.

I remembered whispering to myself, "Life doesn't get any better than this."

Two summers later:

I drive up to a barbed wire fence in a dusty Ford pickup truck and leave the radio blasting on a rural Christian music station. I walk to the middle of a barren, dead pasture, wearing a faded old tee shirt, stained and torn Levis that even Goodwill would not accept, and pink and green floral rubber boots dotted here and there with manure. A floppy, worn out straw hat is protecting my face from the blazing noontime sun, and a sopping wet bath towel is draped around my neck. The cool water dripping down the front and back of my shirt is a welcomed relief from the sweat rolling down to meet it.

I bend down over a big pile of buffalo diarrhea, which I carefully scoop into one of my mother's prized jam jars. I laugh thinking how to tell her its final purpose. I put the jar and its mushy contents in the middle of a plastic container of ice to keep it cool. I look over at three buffalo and a donkey staring at me, clearly wondering why I am determined to retrieve such an odd, smelly package. Being fluent in buffalo and donkey mind reading, I respond, "I am getting a sample of your poop, Billy darlin'. I am hoping we'll find a bunch of worms in it because then we will give you some medicine, and you'll be good as new. Okay, I am off to the lab."

As I close the gate to leave, Buffalo Billy starts walking toward me. I wait for him at the gate and take out the last carrots from my pocket. As he stands in front of me I tell him, "I'd like to stay, Honey, but I have to get this to the vet right away, but I'll be back in time for your dinner." I hold the carrots out for him, and he gently takes them from my hand. I pat his dusty face as he is chomping on the carrots and add, "I love you Billy. We are going to get you well. I promise you that." I bend over his face and he holds his head up for a kiss. I chuckle at the red lipstick kiss mark I leave adorning his brown, crusty nose.

My lifelong dream had come true: to have a bonded relationship with a male buffalo. I felt overwhelmingly happy, content, and completely in the sweaty moment.

I smiled thinking about the last time I had felt this much joy. It was when I was wandering the grounds at Louis' house, but now my life had taken a mischievous detour in a polar opposite direction. I now possessed a new, simpler yet even bigger kind of happiness and lifestyle that I had never imagined for myself. I whispered to Billy, "There is nothing better than this...nothin' better than you and me."

A few weeks before, I had asked for something big to a God who could deliver. Oh boy, did He deliver.

Buffalo Passion

It all began with a passion for buffalo. I don't know exactly where it came from. I can't quite put my finger on when the buffalo bug bit me. But bite me it did, in such a way that it stayed in my blood. I wanted to know everything about these elusive, mammoth creatures, so I studied over the years and became a virtual walking buffalo encyclopedia. I wanted to have buffalo in my life, so I would travel to Yellowstone National Park to admire the herds. The Yellowstone bison are one of the last true, uncontaminated DNA American Bison. In the early 1800's an estimated 20 to 60 million bison roamed the continent. Sadly today, because of the Great Buffalo Slaughter which brought them to the brink of extinction, the approximately 3500 Yellowstone bison are also the only free roaming wild herd left in the US.

40,000 slaughtered buffalo hides from 1878 Dodge City, Kansas

On Christmas in 2006, our neighbors, Rich and Tina Parkman, gave me the perfect gift: the book, *A Buffalo in the House* by RD Rosen. It is the unique story about Roger Brooks, his artist wife Veryl Goodnight, and their pet buffalo, Charlie. After I opened the book on Christmas morning, I ravenously read it cover to cover, making Christmas dinner several hours late. I was living my buffalo dream vicariously through the book. Roger Brooks was fortunate enough to have a trusting relationship with a buffalo, one where you could touch him, hand feed him and be with him without a fence between. Roger and Charlie had a deep bond that was touching and unique, and the true nature of buffalo shined through in their special story.

However make no mistake, bison are wild animals. According to Dr. Jared Diamond, a Pulitzer Prize winning scholar and author, the required traits that enable an animal to be domesticated are not all present in bison. They may be able to be tamed to a point, but their wild nature can never be domesticated. This makes bison, also commonly called buffalo, unpredictable and therefore dangerous. I have had buffalo experts tell me they are "killers." However, my own experience and observation indicates that they are not interested in bothering you, unless and until you make a nuisance or fool out of yourself and bother them.

Bison are the largest land mammals in North America, and healthy adults have no predators. When a creature has this much security in power and size advantage, there is no reason to waste energy being a bully. Considering their weight of 1000-2000 lbs., their potentially lethal pointy horns, the ability to outrun a quarter horse at 35 miles an hour, then turn on a time and jump six ft. in the air...nobody but a fool is going to mess with a bison.

Buffalo treat each other in ways we would consider rough. But with their tough hides, thick hair-cushioned heads, and durable bulk, they are sturdy survivors. However, if they should hook you with a horn or butt you with their head, what means no real harm when done to each other, could easily be a deathblow to you. A 1500 lb. buffalo standing on top of you, for example, would look down at you and curiously wonder why you were screaming so loudly?

Being close to buffalo means always being cautious. Knowing your place is imperative if you want to survive around them. Many fools and the most macho of men have learned a painful or even tragic lesson. Many men have tried to live my dream and Roger's reality and have not lived to tell about it.

I wanted to contact Roger after reading the book. I felt a kinship to him, as we shared many of the same beliefs about buffalo, many contrary to popular fact and opinion. We both felt deeply about the need for respect and protection for this American Icon from our country's past. This is especially true of the bison in Yellowstone National Park, who are caught in the middle of a political, cultural, and agricultural battle not of their own making but to their peril and demise.

The book had introduced me to Roger, a man of few words, who didn't have the interest or the time for small talk. As much as I wanted to contact him with so much I wanted to discuss, for some reason I felt it wasn't time. I would wait.

When I see buffalo, I am literally filled with such joy and emotion, the excitement is intoxicating. If I look into their eyes, I see their souls. To hear them "talk" makes me laugh deep down into my own soul. There is nothing I like better than to watch them for hours, which is probably strange to most everyone else because they don't do a whole lot. Mainly they just stand around, look around, and move around. Buffalo do, in fact, a lot of roaming, as the old western song says. The lyrics must have been written by a cowboy, who like me, loved to observe them. But as stagnant and simple as buffalo life sounds, they are far from boring.

In our world, these impressive beasts would be engineers. They don't do anything quickly, they ponder everything thoroughly, and each one has a mind of its own. They are like elephants, in that they are very sensitive and family bonded. They are like hippopotamus in their mammoth bulk but are like gazelles running gracefully and magically agile. But most amazingly, if you know buffalo, they will teach you everything you need to know about life and yourself. Someday, when we get really smart, we'll have courses where students will "hang" with buffalo for a semester. Crime will be minimal, drug and alcohol addiction nonexistent, wars will be a thing of the past. Buffalo instinctively know everything.

God, how I love buffalo!

My Love Affair with Buffalo Billy

Pray for Something Big

It was the worst of times in 2009. Most of the country was feeling the sting of the recession. For many however, including us, it was more serious. Few people had lived through The Great Depression but there were many similarities. Competent, educated people could not find jobs and the financial markets had crashed along with the stock market. Banks would not lend to the people who had bailed them out and real estate prices had fallen off a cliff, dragging us down with it. My thriving interior design business had practically ground to a halt, and my husband's successful business working with builders almost ceased to exist. It had taken years of hard work and thoughtful planning to build "financial security," but in just six months it was completely wiped out. We were starting over, and we were hurting emotionally as well as financially.

We rented a tiny condo in the Bay area where we worked so we could still hold onto our beautiful country home in Grass Valley, California, where we could escape on the weekends to lick our wounds. The Creekside Paradise was what we called it, and the name described it perfectly. We were willing to sacrifice everything to keep this special place that we had purchased for our retirement ten years prior. But in 2009, early, comfortable retirement went from a certainty to a disillusioned, distant dream.

One late sleepless night, I turned on the TV and began searching for a program for distraction. Pastor Joel Osteen had just begun a sermon about asking God for big things. His logic was that if God can do anything, perform any miracles, why would you ask God for small stuff? Joel reasoned that if we ask Him for big things, He will know we truly believe in Him.

That actually made a lot of sense. I thought if I were a billionaire with unlimited resources and contacts, and if my kid asked me for a rundown trailer to live in, I would be disappointed that he didn't ask me for something better. I would be hurt that my own kid did not think very much of my status and accomplishments. I would think, what is wrong with this kid?!

So that night, not wanting God to think there was something wrong with me, I asked Him for something big. I was not specific about what it would be, but with our bleak circumstances I was thinking in terms of something having to do with business. Little did I know that He would take me so literally. He was not only going to answer my prayer in the biggest way possible, He was going to change my life.

A few weeks after that prayer, I was preparing for my stepson's wedding to be held in our yard by the creek, a perfect setting for a June garden wedding. It was about 4 pm, and I had finished my "to do" list for the day. As I sat relaxing on the island built in the middle of the creek, enjoying the rows of impatiens and the gurgling sound of water, BUFFALO suddenly and inexplicably popped into my mind. A few years before, my husband, Robert, and I went for an afternoon drive and spotted two buffalo in a field. I thought how fun it would be to find them again. I hopped in my car, and being geographically challenged, I headed in some unknown direction I thought we had taken. Somehow my steering wheel took a couple of right turns and began leading me down a windy, pot holed country road that was not at all friendly to older, slow slung Jaguar convertibles. As I scanned the landscape for two large brown figures, I suddenly screeched on the brakes. I spotted three …not two….big, hairy, shaggy, curved horn, chaps-on-their-front-legs buffalo! The male and female I had seen years before had now been joined by a baby. I couldn't believe that after a quick 15-minute drive, I was staring at my passion. I got out of the car and walked to the barbed wire fence to get a better look. They were standing near a barn about 75 yards away. All three buffalo stared at me, staring at them. They certainly weren't as excited about seeing me, as I was about them. They were curious. I was ecstatic. They stood stoic, but I was smiling inside and out.

I stood their gawking, like a rock star groupie. Suddenly a donkey, who I hadn't even noticed, came sauntering up to me, shoving his head between the barbed wire to introduce himself. I had never been close to a donkey before and he was really cute. I said, "Hi" to him and patted his face, but my focus was still on the buffalo. But that donkey was not going to play second fiddle to any-buffalo-body. When I moved to the side so I could see them better, the donkey moved with me. When I tried to look around his face so I could see the buffalo, he stuck his head in front of mine so he would be my focus. If he weren't so entertaining and needy I would have been irritated. Instead, I was not only in the presence of three American Icons, I had just acquired a new donkey best friend forever (DBFF) who was as excited to see me as I was to see the buffalo. I had no idea a donkey could make you feel so special.

I had been to the grocery store a few hours before and still had some produce in my car. I popped the trunk open and fed that adorable donkey greeter some carrots, which he gobbled enthusiastically through big orange colored teeth. I had come to see the buffalo, but this donkey wanted all my attention and all of my carrots. The buffalo remained at a distance, frozen in their iconic stance, and watched everything that my new DBFF and I did.

The next day, I was eager to finish my wedding to do list and go see the buffalo…and my new buddy. As soon as I pulled up, the donkey came a runnin' and belted out an ear deafening "HEE-HAW." He was so happy and excited to see me, and his uneven, legs flopping, silly gait was hilarious to watch. I quickly stuffed the carrots into his mouth in an attempt to protect my eardrums. While he was voraciously chomping, I looked over at the buffalo standing near the barn and shouted, "Hi guys!" which was a pretty lame thing to say to left over prehistoric beasts. But that's how you feel in the presence of buffalo: lame, insignificant, in awe. The magnificent hairy icons remained motionless and continued sizing me up. I guessed I would just have to wait for the roaming part.

I returned every day for a week, for what was becoming a ritual visit. I couldn't wait to go see the buffalo. In doing so I was falling hard for that donkey, even though I was concerned that I was repeatedly subjecting myself to severe hearing loss.

On the eighth visit, as I drove up to the fence, everything was normal: donkey screeching, buffalo staring. When the carrots were all eaten, the donkey positioned himself with his complete left side up against the fence. He was telling me he wanted his side massaged. And so, being a receptive donkey mind reader, I had to oblige. As I was talking to the donkey, while practicing my newly acquired talent as an equine masseuse, I briefly spotted something moving…something big and brown…moving. I looked up over the donkey's shoulder and saw the male buffalo walking toward us! I was both excited and terrified. He kept coming, slowly, step by deliberate step, he just kept coming. My heart was racing. When the buffalo arrived within ten ft. of us, the donkey darted away. After all, a smart donkey's got to know his limitations. I had not yet recognized mine, however. I just stood there feeling very alone, and exposed, and excited, as the buffalo kept walking toward me.

All I could think to say was, "Oh my God," which meant one of my biggest dreams in life was about to come true: to be standing right next to an American Bison. It also meant I could be in serious danger because buffalo are wild and powerful, and that flimsy fence could no more deter a buffalo who wanted out than I could prevent that donkey from screeching. I suppose I held my breath and didn't move away, but I don't remember exactly because I was frozen in both terror and joy. The buffalo walked calmly up to me and the fence, staring me down, but he didn't appear mean or threatening. I unfroze my lips and blurted out, "Hi." He didn't care to answer and kept his gaze fixed on me.

I had given the donkey all of the carrots, but I had some strawberries in the car. Knowing bison eat berries in the wild, I asked him, "Would you like some strawberries?" He didn't say "No," so I slowly walked backward on rubbery, trembling legs, and grabbed a strawberry from the basket, with the buffalo intently watching my every move. Then a troubling thought popped into my head: I have this little strawberry. How am I going to feed it to this huge animal without getting my hand bitten off, or hurt even worse? This momentary trepidation was overcome by my wildest (pun intended) dream, that stood facing me just a few feet away.

I looked at my hand for what I had hoped was not the last time, took a deep breath, and pretended to walk casually up to the buffalo. I said, "Here you are handsome. I hope you like this." (Boy did I mean it) as my frightened fingers held the little strawberry next to a head that was bigger than my torso. I held my breath and hoped for the best. He very gently took the strawberry, chewed it, swallowed it, and then he thrust his entire 200 lb. head through the fence! His scruffy chin was resting on my chest as he looked up at me for more. I had to laugh. It was a lot braver than screaming. I excused myself from being his headrest and went back to the car to get the strawberries. I fed him all the berries, one by one, which he took gratefully and gently.

And that was the start of my love affair with Buffalo Billy.

God had delivered something really big: the biggest land mammal in North America and my biggest impossible dream. The old saying, "Be careful what you ask for," was certainly apropos here. God has a terrific sense of humor.

The next day I brought a big bag of carrots. The donkey ran up to me at the fence and the buffalo stood congregated at their usual place by the barn. As I fed the donkey, I yelled to the buffalo male, "Hi, buddy." "Come have some carrots." He stood motionless for a few minutes, carefully pondering his every decision, and then started walking toward me. The donkey began eating faster to get as many carrots chewed before being evicted from his spot at the fence. When the buffalo reached within ten ft., the donkey kicked up his back legs in defiant protest and then cowardly ran like crazy. The buffalo came up to the fence, and I put a carrot up to his mouth, he opened it, and I put it right in. He enjoyed the carrot, and I hand fed him the rest. Meanwhile, the mom and baby buffalo looked on from the barn but didn't make a move. The entire time I was feeding the dad, I was jabbering away as he looked at me with big, calm, accepting brown eyes. When the carrots were all eaten, I asked him if he wanted some grass. I noticed nothing was growing in their enclosure but inedible weeds (called Mountain Misery for a reason) and it was covered with feces. I walked across the street and pulled off some of the tall grasses, which the buffalo eagerly, but gently, ate from my hand. I told him how thrilled I was to be feeding him, and that he was exceptionally handsome. He silently listened to every word and seemed to enjoy the company and the attention, not to mention the treats.

In the week that followed, I continued to feed the donkey and the male buffalo carrots and the grasses I pulled off the hill. However, my initial excitement to see the buffalo blinded me to the fact that they, and the donkey too, were painfully thin, and the buffalo's coats were not shedding properly for the start of summer. The male was the worst looking. One day he turned away from me, and I saw him from behind. I was shocked at his bony rear end. It looked pitifully like skin draped over a skeleton. I began to be concerned, seeing nothing to eat in the pasture and no evidence of hay left out for them. This minimal amount I was feeding him was not even close to meeting his needs. I decided to go to a feed store to purchase some nutritious grass hay.

My black Jaguar convertible had been my pride and joy. I had lusted over that car when it was first introduced, and the day I drove it out of the dealership was one of the happiest and most fulfilling days of my life. But now it was a 6 year old, 110,000 mile, dirty, reddish brown/black car from all the dust that had accumulated from my visits to feed the animals. As I drove into the "drive through" of the feed store, everyone turned to look. Unfortunately it wasn't my good looks that intrigued them. I guessed they had never before had the privilege of seeing a Jaguar convertible double as a hay wagon. A cute blonde cowgirl came up to my car window and said, "How can I help you?"

I said in my most matter of fact voice, "Oh, I just need a bale of grass hay."

Standing next to her was the owner, Mark, a friendly rancher type, who was trying hard not to laugh. He said, "And where are you going to put it?"

I jumped out of the car and said, "In here," as I popped open the trunk.

Mark couldn't hold back any longer and laughed. "Well, I have never seen a luxury hay wagon before. What are you feeding…horses?"

I said proudly, "Buffalo!"

Mark had a partner who once owned some buffalo in Grass Valley, and had taken care of them from time to time. So, we "talked buffalo," he added in a little cowboy small talk, and I drove off. I watched in my rear view mirror how everyone got a good chuckle at the expense of my beloved, dusty, hay filled, luxury feed wagon. Well at least we gave them a good laugh, and they definitely wouldn't forget us.

That evening, the hay wagon and I went to feed "The Kids", as I began to call them. As usual, the donkey ran to me as fast as his goofy gait would take him to get a stuffed mouthful of carrots before being bullied off. The buffalo male trailed behind at his own deliberate pace. I hand fed the gentle giant some of the healthy grass hay, which he greedily ate. Then I threw a pile of hay on the ground in front of him. He looked at me. He slowly looked down at the hay, and then looked back up at me, and just stood there. Clearly he was not about to eat his food off the ground after being hand fed! I quickly realized an apology was in order so I said, "I am sorry, Sweetie. I don't know what I was thinking." I then held out a clump of hay, which he happily ate from my hand. I was spoiling him by hand feeding him and he had let me know it was now expected. I laughed and told him I loved doing it for him.

Who would believe it? I was hand feeding a buffalo! And not just because it had always been my dream, but because he wanted it that way. And who is going to argue with a wild, unpredictable animal with sharp horns standing in front of you?

After a while, the mother buffalo started walking toward me with the baby in tow. I was so thrilled that she might give me a chance for her trust. But she suddenly turned around and headed back toward the barn, then she paced to the side, stopped, and trotted toward me. I coaxed the male over a few feet with some hay, and she began to eat the grass I had thrown on the ground. She would not let the baby come forward to get near me, and she ate all of the grass as if it were her last meal. I threw another big pile of hay down for her. Finally, with enough food on the ground, she let her baby come closer. I was surprised that she let the baby come within ten ft. of me, as buffalo moms are fiercely protective and doting, and this one was skittish and nervous by nature. I remained cautious as the family ate their dinner together, while I was their ever efficient server.

Soon a car pulled up to the driveway, and a bearded man in his early 60's opened the door. He walked over to the mailbox, and I walked toward him asking, "Are these your animals?"

He said that they were. I introduced myself and asked him if he was okay with me feeding them. I explained that bison were a real passion of mine, and I had studied them for many years. His name was Gary and he told me he was happy that I was feeding them and that I got so much joy from it. I told him I was the editor of the community newspaper, and that I wanted to write an article about his buffalo. Gary was excited about having his animals in the paper. We exchanged phone numbers, and I told him I would call him for an interview and photo session. Gary told me that the male's name was Buffalo Bill, the female was Napini, meaning "wife" in his mother's native Choctaw language. They named the baby, Minko, which Gary said meant "Duke." Evidently, Minko had not had the opportunity to show what a beautiful little femme fatale she was before she was mistakenly associated with John Wayne. Mr. Hee-Haw was called Whiskey.

At the Buffalo Grazing Party, friends gather at the fence to meet
Billy and watch him enjoy his rice bran pellet treats from his "special plate".

Billy's Coming Out Party

I thought it would be a fun idea to have a Buffalo Grazing Party. I wanted to share my new buffalo experience with my friends, and I wanted Billy to have even more admirers.

I invited all of our good friends to do something they would never have the opportunity to do in a lifetime: to be up close and personal, and perhaps hand feed a bison. I knew Napini and Minko would not come to the fence with so many strangers, but if I were there, I knew Billy would come.

Gary had told me he was going through a rough time in his life. I thought the idea of having a party, where he would be the center of attention surrounded by fun and kind people, would lift his spirits. So I asked Gary for permission to have a cocktail party at our house and later, we would all go to his house to feed the animals. Of course, he would be the guest of honor.

Gary agreed to the idea, and during the party, our conversation was mainly "talking buffalo." I told my story about praying for something big, and we all drank a toast to God and big prayers.

After our cocktails and appetizers, one of which was cheese cut into the shape of buffalo heads, we loaded the truck with carrots and hay and drove to Billy's Place. When we arrived, the bison stood stoically by the barn, watching everyone emerge from their cars. They were used to visitors stopping, but this was something new. Whiskey, however, recognizing a party when he saw one, raced toward us for carrots and attention. He expressed his party attitude with his screeching, yet crowd pleasing HEE-HAW.

I yelled, "Billeeee! Come see your Auntie!" and he started walking. Everyone was amazed that a buffalo would come when he was called. I was beaming with pride and excitement, watching this immense creature walking toward me.

As I fed Billy carrots, Napini and Minko walked warily behind him and stood 20 ft. away, unsure of what they should do. I said, "Hi, Sweet Boy. Look at all these people who came to meet you!" Billy was casually sizing up his admirers as he ate the carrots. One of my friends very tentatively held out some hay through the fence, not sure if she really wanted this wild animal so close. Billy decided, "Why not give her a thrill?" and took the hay gently. She laughed in astonishment and immediately had that stupid grin and elation on her face that only an encounter with a buffalo can put there.

Everyone was feeding Whiskey and he was in his glory with all the attention and not having to compete with Napini for food. Napini kept her distance and gave us a look of, "Don't you people have better things to do? Go home! I'm hungry!" Not only was she not a party animal, she was also a real party pooper.

Our friends were commenting quietly about the bare pasture covered with poop, and the tragedy of so many flies annoying the animals. The flies were crawling all around their eyes, and it made everyone uncomfortable to see it. But not as uncomfortable as it made the poor animals.

I had purchased some fly repellent spray at the feed store and said to Gary, "The flies are a problem with any big animals and I am concerned that they might get eye infections from the flies landing on the feces and then on their eyes. It would be a real challenge trying to administer eye medication to a buffalo." Gary nodded and chuckled with me about that.

I said, "I've purchased some fly spray I'll give you." Gary said he could put it into a sprayer that he had. I asked him if he would try spraying the animals first. I didn't know how they would react to it, and I didn't want Billy upset with me. Gary laughed and said he would let me know how it went. I told him it was recommended to spray them weekly, and I would be willing to help with it.

The Buffalo Grazing Party was a big success, and everyone, animal and human, had a great time. However, Napini had a much better time after we all left. She could eat in peace without all the gawkers, and she could resume her favorite pastime....bullying poor Whiskey away from the food. Whiskey hated to see the party end, and walked with us down to the very end of the fencing, hoping for some last minute carrot treats he could gobble down without provocation. When it was clear the party was over, we were given a friendly HEE-HAW send off, as our ears rang all the way home.

Jumping In With Both Feet For Billy

Gary mentioned during the Buffalo Grazing Party that he had purchased the buffalo when they were six months old from a ranch in southern California. Since his mother was Native American, he thought it would be fun to own buffalo. But the real motive, as he explained it, was to have them graze down his two-plus acre field so he wouldn't have to mow it. Obviously the buffalo did their job well, because since he also wasn't watering it, there was not one blade of grass. Only the aptly named "Mountain Misery" weeds could survive the harsh conditions, and neither Whiskey nor the buffalo would touch it, no matter how hungry they were.

But even a lawn mower needs fuel. To turn wild animals out in a small enclosure and expect them to fend for themselves defies common sense. Three large grazers, and an additional big baby, would denude the land of forage in no time, especially in a climate with no summer rainfall. It was a perplexing situation since there was, in fact, an irrigation system fed by a well on the property. For some reason Gary wouldn't turn it on. If you confine four large animals to this kind of environment, then you have to feed them.

With the buffalo being no more than skin and bones, and with them eating what I brought them as if they hadn't eaten in days, I decided to ask Gary how much he was feeding them. I had to compose myself with his reply, "Oh, I throw out a couple flakes a day."

Hay is compressed into one bale from eight to ten smaller clumps. Each clump can be separated from the bale and are called flakes. Based on their ideal weight, these four animals would need about ten flakes a day for proper nutrition, not the two Gary said he gave them.

Poor Billy was suffering the brunt of it. Gary had told me how Billy would allow Napini, to eat first while he would wait. I am sure it was partly due to her exasperating, pushy nature. However, all living creatures will fight over food, especially if they are starving. Billy clearly had the advantage of size over Napini, and she would defer to him when challenged. Yet the heart wrenching fact was that this sensitive, gentle giant was putting himself at risk so his mate and baby could survive. I was so moved by Billy's choice to defy the most basic of survival instincts, and I began to realize the inevitable and tragic outcome of his decision. I chose to jump in with both feet and help Billy, his family, and their donkey sidekick. Billy had trusted me and I could not let him down. Nor could I ignore that he had been the answer to my big prayer. Perhaps I was the answer to his.

I drove away thinking, "How am I going to tell Gary that the animals need five times more food than what he is giving them without offending him? He had owned the bison for six years and must have known their nutritional requirements. Perhaps when they arrived at six months of age, the property was full of tall grass and was watered to keep it growing. But even if the water were turned on and natural grass began to grow, this small field could not sustain these three and a half large animals.

Gary had told me his wife had left him, his business was in shambles and he wasn't working. I sympathized with him and shared our own financial position so he would not feel alone. Perhaps he was so distressed that he did not realize the state of his animals. I felt sorry for him, but I felt sorrier for the animals, who were trapped and completely helpless. It made me sad to think that bison, our American symbol of strength and independence, were struggling to survive in an unnatural and unhealthy environment with a meager handout of a few mouthfuls of food.

The next afternoon, Gary was happy to see me drive up with several bales of hay in our truck, and he came out to the fence to chat. I was just about to discuss the food issue, when a car pulled up with a blonde lady inside. She got out of the car, came over to the fence and called to Billy. Gary introduced me to his estranged wife as I handed her some carrots to feed Billy. After looking at him closely she said, "Gary, Bill looks awful. Haven't you been feeding them?"

Gary replied, "Well maybe I should throw out more hay." I later learned that, ironically, Gary's soon-to-be ex was on the board of an animal rescue group.

After she left, it was the perfect opportunity to tell Gary about the food requirements. When I told him the animals needed ten flakes a day, he seemed a bit perturbed. I told him I would be willing to supply half their food needs and feed them in the late afternoon, if he would feed them the other half in the morning. Gary said, "That would be great. I would really appreciate it." He then offered me the combination to his locked entry gate so I could use his barn. I had been lugging the food every day in my Jaguar convertible turned hay wagon, or the truck when Robert was home, so I was grateful to be able to store the feed in his barn.

After receiving advice about putting weight on the animals, I first added rice bran pellets to their diet, with Gary's knowledge and consent. I had figured out a way to feed it to them, rather than just throwing it on the ground. I had a very large plastic dish designed to hold water under an outside garden pot that was sturdy enough and large enough to serve as a buffalo's plate. My plan was to fill it with the rice bran pellets and put it on the ground for them. The only problem with my plan was, Billy didn't like it. His plan was for me to hold the plate for him just under his chin while he ate from it. I obliged, of course, but since his head literally weighed more than I did, it was difficult holding it up and holding onto it. If his weighty head tilted his plate downward and the pellets spilled on the ground, he would usually wait patiently until I refilled it. Napini, on the other hand, would be right in there gobbling up the pellets, trying to push everyone else out of the way.

When I fed The Kids, I left their food piled on the berm next to the fence, which was the only place that wasn't covered with feces. I wanted to discuss with Gary that where he was feeding the animals was exposing them to the threat of parasites, or worms as they are commonly called.

According to Gary, he threw out their food under a metal awning where the ground was thick with manure....even worse than the rest of the pasture. However, the worst area was a room-sized pile, two ft. high and growing of donkey manure. Poor Whiskey was doing his best trying to contain it.

Parasites or worms come from feces. If animals eat food that has come in contact with feces, they will get parasites. The worm larvae will be ingested with the food and the worms feed on the lining of their host's digestive system. The animal's immune system is alerted to this invasion, and goes to work to repair the damage by forming calluses to fill in the holes in the stomach lining eaten away by the parasites. But if worms continue their ghastly feast unchecked, the calluses build up to such a point that nutrients are prevented from passing through the stomach lining to the body, resulting in the animal slowly starving to death. It takes over 20,000 worms to kill a bison. The thought of those horrible creatures eating The Kids alive was unbearable.

As horrible as they are, parasites can be easily eliminated by using over the counter dewormers available at any feed store. No animal should ever die from common parasites.

There is a theory that cattle, being domesticated and confined, have built up a better tolerance for parasites than bison, whose historic nature was to eat and roam for miles, keeping them away from a buildup of feces.

With the unhealthy conditions at Billy's Place, it was a sure bet that the animals had parasites, and their emaciated condition was further evidence.

I asked Gary if he had ever dewormed the animals. He said that Billy and Napini had only been dewormed before arriving at his place six years ago. I suggested that the reason they were so thin was due to parasites, and they should be dewormed as soon as possible. I did not want to offend Gary, nor did I want to be perceived as someone eager to tell him what to do. I thought he must be overwhelmed with his problems and I did not want to become another one. However, he seemed to appreciate my knowledge about buffalo and my advice, along with caring for them. I believed that he wanted the best for his "pets" as he called them. Anyone who referred to buffalo as pets was okay by me.

Our American Icon, The Buffalo

Bison were critical to the health of the Great Plains, and as the keystone animal, they provided everything necessary to keep the plant and animal life flourishing. Buffalo graze the land by eating only the tops of the forage and by constantly roaming, so the land is not adversely disturbed and grass/forage continues to grow. The Great Plains was generously fertilized by their manure and was replanted from seeds collected on their coats. Bison wallowing holes retained water from rainstorms providing drinking holes for all animals. The prairie dogs and other ground dwellers relied on the buffalo tilling the soil with their heavy hooves. The old, young, and sickly provided food for large predators and scavengers, and even in death, buffalo replenished the land with their decaying bodies. They sustained entire cultures of indigenous peoples, whose very existence relied on using every part of the buffalo. Even their religious practices included the iconic beasts.

When the pioneers and settlers moved west, the land was what they came for...land that was centuries owned and divided into territories by tribes of Native Americans. As settlers began to take the land for themselves, the US government introduced titles to it, to justify the land grab and make it legal. The tribes naturally fought back, for what had been their ancestral land.

The US government and others encouraged the extermination of the bison. If the buffalo were gone, the American Indians could not survive. It was an ethnic cleansing our government perpetuated and nearly won, as it is estimated that 90% of the indigenous peoples were wiped out. The bison were innocent bystanders in this effort and were used to solve a problem by means of their own extermination. The bond between the Indians and the buffalo had played out for centuries, and it was to bind them to their deaths and near extinction for both.

Buffalo have roamed the earth for over 10,000 years and were one of the few remaining dinosaurs tough enough to evolve and survive. In less than a decade in the late 1800's, their numbers in the tens of millions were reduced to several dozen. They were not tough enough to survive millions of bullets from Winchester rifles, the white man's greed for land, and the hatred and intolerance of people whose culture was different and therefore deemed worthless. The cruel plan for the Indians they could not kill was to supply them with alcohol, which their bodies could not chemically tolerate, and to wipe out the buffalo. If they didn't die off from starvation or fade away from alcohol abuse, they would be imprisoned on reservations on unfamiliar, remote and uninhabitable lands. We condemn other countries for historic human rights violations, yet our own shameful history of oppression of the American Indian is rife with horror. And with it, the tragedy of the Great Buffalo Slaughter is entwined.

But as bad as the options were for the Native Americans imprisoned on reservations, the buffalo's only option was death. So a campaign ensued for the slaughter of millions upon millions of American Bison.

The skulls of millions of slaughtered buffalo in the late 1800's

Fashion became enthralled with buffalo skins and epicureans licked their lips for sautéed buffalo tongues. The railroad needed meat for their mountain of workers, and the entertaining sport of shooting buffalo from train windows was all the rage. The Great Buffalo Slaughter was so successful that pioneers reported that it was nearly impossible to see land on the plains that wasn't scattered thick with bleached buffalo bones. So they found a use for the bones....in fertilizer.

Bison were regarded as stupid and easy marks. However healthy adult bison have no predators to fear, and their nature is to be closely family bonded, staying within a herd. So "brave" marksmen would find a comfortable place to lie down near a herd and proceed with the massacre. One by one the buffalo fell by each other's side. This carnage would continue all day, every day, until herd after herd were exterminated. Reports surfaced that the buffalo were savage and would attack their fallen brothers. The so-called attack was actually disconsolate grief, trying to revive their dead brothers, mothers, and children. In Yellowstone Park for example, buffalo advocates from the Buffalo Field Campaign have videoed bison bachelor groups sensitively stopping and waiting, or even returning for their comrades, that have been injured running from government hazing efforts to confine them within the Park.

In RD Rosen's book, *A Buffalo in the House*, pioneer Mary Anne Goodnight recalled how she could not bear the constant gunshots she heard every day from buffalo being shot and killed in the nearby canyons. Mary Anne Goodnight saved the buffalo from complete extinction in Texas, pleading with her husband to bring some to their ranch for safety. In addition, about two dozen bison were saved near Yellowstone, where they were taken into the park to escape the relentless hunting, and where their descendants survive today. Without the efforts of a handful of people who recognized the buffalo tragedy and their willingness to take action to prevent their extinction, we would only speak of buffalo now as a myth from our country's past.

Few people know that the Great Buffalo Slaughter directly contributed to one of the world's worst ecological disasters….the Dust Bowl of the early 1900's. The Great Plains stretched from Mexico into Canada with the bison being the primary environmental caretaker. When the bison were gone, cattlemen and farmers moved in, not realizing it was a landscape of historic climatic shifts, not well suited for the exploitation imposed by both.

Eventually, the cattle industry failed, as cattle were ill-suited for the harsh, changing conditions, and as the prolific buffalo grass began to be plowed under for crops, the end result was ten years of blowing dust, lives and livelihoods lost, and a previously healthy landscape converted into nothing but a barren desert.

What the government allowed and destroyed the government was required to restore. New methods of farming were developed and millions of dollars of scarce depression era funds were spent to turn the desolation of the once fertile Great Plains into habitability again. However, no attempt was made to bring back the very thing nature had provided to enrich and protect the prairie. Still we continued to ignore and devalue the prairie's natural salvation….the American Bison.

The cruelty, savagery and lack of understanding toward our very symbol of freedom and perseverance is a deep, historic, national shame. What's worse, it is still happening. There are only about 3500 true DNA wild buffalo surviving today that are still being killed outside of Yellowstone National Park. . . . hunting or slaughter sanctioned and encouraged by our government. True DNA bison owned by us, the citizens of the United States, also on other national lands are being sold off to slaughter or an unknown future without our understanding and consent. Once the invaluable genetics of that animal finally rests on a dinner plate for a forgettable 15-minute meal, it is gone forever. The question begs, why are these national icons not protected?

The buffalo's tragic story had always deeply moved me. While I could do nothing to right their painful past, I could do something to save these three who had captured my heart.

The American Bison Patient

I loved the buffalo and Whiskey more each day, and I was haunted by the certainty that they were suffering from parasites. Not only were the animals painfully thin, but they also had diarrhea. Poor Billy had it the worst. When I finally did see him poop, it was like water shooting out of a fire hose, and I knew he needed immediate help.

I asked Gary if I could locate a veterinarian to come treat Billy. I told him I would call the veterinary school at UC Davis first, since they would be the best source to locate a bison vet. I explained that because they were a teaching school, perhaps we might be able to receive treatment at no cost. I did not know for certain if that was a possibility, but I wanted Gary to agree to have a vet see Billy. The school recommended three veterinarians, but none from the university and all without any substantial experience with bison. They told me one woman did have some contact with bison from a vet school she attended in Wyoming, so I called her first. I explained the situation over the phone, and she told me to call back to arrange an appointment. She seemed uncomfortable that I was not the animal's owner, even when I assured her that he would be there for her visit. After several calls to her went unreturned, I moved on. I could not waste any time, considering Billy's tenuous condition. After two days of calling and receiving referrals from other vets, I arranged an appointment for what was described as a "ruminate vet" to come evaluate the animals. Bison are ruminates, but so are cattle, goats and deer. What they have in common is multi-chambered stomachs, but the management and dietary needs of various ruminates are not the same. I didn't feel good about the vet's lack of experience with bison, but at least it would be a start, and I could later contact experts from around the country for further advice.

The state veterinarian of South Dakota, Dr. Dustin Oedekoven, works with bison on a regular basis. I contacted him, and he kindly responded with some advice and even offered to take a look at them, not realizing I was in California. I contacted several other bison ranchers, and one woman coldly told me the common mantra for sick buffalo, "If buffalo get sick, they die." I hung up the phone determined to prove her and this defeatist attitude wrong. I felt sorry for ranchers who are fortunate enough to have such incredible animals, yet never bother to really know them. To them, they are just livestock…an expendable commodity.

I had read an interesting presentation about parasites in bison from Dr. Murray Woodbury from the Western College of Veterinary Medicine at the University of Saskatchewan. In Canada, there are also the endangered wood bison, a cousin to Billy's plains bison. Dr. Woodbury was the University Chair of Specialized Livestock Research and Production. I sent him an e-mail describing The Kids affliction, the circumstances of why I was involved, and asked for help. Dr. Woodbury questioned why I was feeding someone else's animals and warned that I might put in all the effort and expense, only to end up getting burned. Dr. Woodbury had the wisdom and experience to judiciously size up any situation, and the boldness to articulate it. Not only did he have the invaluable experience that I needed with bison, he had the heart to match….a combination that made him uniquely and exceedingly effective.

I explained to Dr. Woodbury that I was aware of my awkward and tenuous situation with the bison's owner, but that it didn't matter. It wasn't about me, and it wasn't about the owner; it was about saving the animals. I thought of the expression related to the Holocaust that cut through to the quick of every moral question: "If not me, who? If not now, when?" I could not walk away from these three precious American treasures or from a donkey with a voice that had pierced my heart. Because Dr. Woodbury realized that I was going to take care of the animals no matter what he said to discourage me, he generously agreed to share his knowledge. He was caring in a firm, direct, no nonsense way, and I trusted him completely.

Dr. Woodbury was the white knight we so desperately needed. From 1800 miles away, he would give free medical advice to a perfect stranger. He would take the time to warn me about the dangers of working with bison, and he cared about how this would turn out for me and the animals. I had no greater friend, and the buffalo had no greater advocate than this hero I knew only as typed letters on my computer.

While I had a lot of book knowledge about bison, I rarely articulated it. I was interested in listening to others so I could learn more. Most of the time, I would listen to people who basically knew nothing about what they were saying, and whose advice could have been detrimental had I followed it. I evaluated each piece of advice carefully based on what I already knew, and continued to do research and to contact the real experts, like Dr. Woodbury. I had no experience in bringing sick bison back to health. The frustration came with the lack of sound knowledge due to so little research relating to bison health. There are lots of theories but so little is actually known.

I decided to obtain a poop sample from Billy and find a lab to test for parasites. That way, when the vet arrived, we would be that much ahead for a diagnosis and treatment for Billy and The Kids. I located a clinic about 40 miles away and confirmed I would be in that day with a bison fecal sample.

When I got to Billy's Place, The Kids were taking their afternoon naps hidden behind some boulders in the back hill area. I yelled, "Billeeee", and a big, hairy, horned head popped up above a rock. He looked surprised to see me there so early in the day. I could tell he was thinking, "Is it dinner time already?" I looked around for a fresh pile of runny poop, to no avail.

I said, "Come here, Angel. I need you to poop for me." Billy slowly got up and the whole gang lumbered over, curious about what was so important that I had to disturb their naps. I had a bag of carrots and apples, which I fed mostly to Billy. I began to break the news to him gently, "Honey, I have a bit of bad news. I think you've got some nasty parasites." Billy listened and looked intently into my eyes as I continued, "But the good news is, if they are in your poop, it means we can kill those nasty suckers and you will get well. But don't you worry Billy, your Auntie is going to make sure you get well. I promise you that. So do you think you can muster up a little buffalo patty for me?" Billy stood a minute thinking about it. I said, "I know it doesn't bother you too much standing in the sun with 100 degree heat, but I am roasting!" The sweat was pouring off the band of my hat, my bra, the waist of my pants, and my socks were steaming in my rubber boots. Billy soon obliged his Auntie and stepped back to deposit a big plop of runny poop.

Billy was clearly bored with discussing his health issues and was ready to finish his nap. He turned to head back up the hill, and his entourage followed. I opened the gate, ran for the poop pile, scooped it up in my mother's jam jar, surrounded by a plastic bag filled with ice to keep it fresh, and drove off, over the speed limit to the clinic.

When I arrived, the receptionist knew who I was. They evidently do not get a lot of calls to test buffalo poop. A technician overheard my conversation about Billy, and as she took my cool, brown colored glass jar she said, "Usually if there is bad diarrhea, it's too late for treatment." I gasped, whipped my head around and stared so hard at her, it almost knocked her over.

The receptionist tried to smooth over the gaff by saying, "Well that is true with some animals but not necessarily with bison," and she stared just as hard at the technician to stop her from talking further.

All the way home, those ugly words were playing reruns in my head. But I reminded myself that most people don't know about bison. Billy IS going to get better. I promised him that. He will get better. He WILL get well!

The phone rang the next day and it was the clinic. The ruminate vet who was coming to see Billy, Dr. Mario, was not available. A horse vet was calling me, since I had insisted that I be notified as soon as the lab tests were evaluated. The vet told me that since there wasn't a large presence of worms, we should probably look to some other explanation for Billy's illness. She proceeded to tell me every bad scenario, every potentially bad outcome known to buffalo. Of course, she said she was a horse vet, and Dr. Mario would know better. I hung up the phone and cried.

In the back of my mind, as far back as I could push it, I had been concerned about a condition called Johnes disease. (pronounced Yo-Knees) Johnes disease is commonly referred to as the wasting disease. Buffalo never suffered from it until cattle were introduced to the plains and infected them with it. The disease is highly infectious in young ruminants, untreatable, and ultimately fatal. The animal slowly wastes away by starving to death because the inflamed intestines can't absorb nutrients. Johnes is similar to Chron's disease in humans. If Billy had Johnes disease, it was certain that The Girls also had it, and there would be a high probability that other ruminates in the area could also be infected. There could be no worse affliction than this dreaded disease for buffalo. Whenever the horrific thought of Billy possibly having Johnes crept into my mind, I fought to keep it back. Instead, I thought we'd find what was wrong with him and cure it. Billy did NOT have Johnes. His Auntie would not allow it.

Dr. Mario was standing at the barn admiring The Kids when I drove up for the appointment. He was a thirty something clean cut cowboy, dressed for the part of a ruminate vet. I introduced him to Billy and The Girls, and Whiskey introduced himself in his usual eardrum blasting way. I yelled to Dr. Mario, "Sorry, I forgot to tell you to bring ear protection!" He chuckled and dismissed it. Evidently this was just one of the hazards of the job and unfortunately not even covered by workers' comp.

The vet was definitely concerned about the animal's health and Billy's in particular. He thought Billy was 300 lbs. underweight and recommended feeding them only grass hay with limited treats until their diarrhea subsided. I asked him to please tell their owner how much the animals needed to eat. I was certain if Gary heard it directly from a vet he would heed it. I knew he cared about his animals but was just in a bad way. Dr. Mario explained that even though there were not a lot of worms in Billy's poop sample, it didn't mean there was not a parasite problem. He explained sometimes a sample would not show a lot of parasites because of where they are in the digestive system. He looked out at the condition of their enclosure and confirmed it was a parasite haven.

I walked up to the house to bring Gary down to meet Dr. Mario. The vet explained that there was no food for the animals to eat in their pasture, and they had to be fed. He said they needed ten flakes a day and recommended five in the morning and five in the evening. He told Gary that with the current condition of the pasture and with no pasture management of feces, parasites would be a constant health threat. Dr. Mario said we should deworm the animals now, and that their diarrhea should subside in a week. He also said if the pasture continued in this condition, the animals would need to be dewormed every three months.

Gary handed him a squeeze tube of dewormer that he had purchased. In cattle, you open their mouths and squirt a dose in. No one would be crazy enough to try that with bison. Dr. Mario was pondering how we might accomplish administering the medication and said, "We could mix it with some food."

I said, "Great! They love rice bran pellets and we could mix it in with the pellets. Or we could also mix it with apples or carrots." I pointed to my car, "I have it all in my trunk."

Dr. Mario said incredulously, "In THAT trunk?" Everyone always underestimated my sleek Jaguar convertible as a buffalo utility vehicle. It was amazing how much I could pack in that trunk, and being able to take the top down provided even more stacking room. I popped the trunk open to reveal big bags of carrots and apples, a 25 lb. bag of rice bran pellets, and a half a bale of alfalfa.

Dr. Mario recommended mixing the dewormer with the pellets. So with the only utensils I had, I mixed the pasty dewormer and the pellets with my hands. Dr. Mario said, "Now, how are we going to feed it to them?"

I picked up Billy's Plate from my passenger seat and said, "That's easy… in Billy's Plate. He will only eat rice bran pellets off this plate." Dr. Mario and Gary shook their heads and laughed. I knew they were both thinking, "I've got to see this!"

I walked over to Billy, who had been watching everything from the barn gate. "Hi, Honey. Here is your medicine. Be good now and eat it so you will get well." Billy moved right up to the plate I held out for him, and he lapped up the gooey dewormer and pellets with his tongue. His head was turned to the side, and he was looking up at me as I was thanking him and telling him how special he was. Dr. Mario then tossed the thick medicine paste to Napini and Minko and fed it to Whiskey. Some of Billy's paste fell on the ground, and Nappy was right there to lap it up. Dr. Mario was concerned that Billy didn't get enough, and the tube had more left in it. He said, "I think I can do this." He walked over to Billy, held the tube up to his mouth, Billy opened up, and Dr. Mario squirted it down his throat. And just like that, Billy swallowed it without hesitation or objection. We were all standing with our mouths grinning open in awe. Dr. Mario laughed and said, "Why should we be surprised? His Auntie here practically taught him how to do it!"

Gary was laughing too and said, "I swear she can get that buffalo to do anything."

I felt so bad that I had doubted my precious boy. After all, he did exactly what I had asked him to do. He was the perfect patient, the ultimate friend, and the best buffalo that ever lived.

I had not been convinced that I should be feeding the buffalo only grass hay. They were so emaciated that it would take a long time to gain weight with hay alone, and I felt their health would continue to be in jeopardy. I decide to turn to the real expert, my computer type friend, Dr. Woodbury.

When I e-mailed Dr. Woodbury and explained that Dr. Mario estimated that Billy was three hundred pounds underweight, he replied, "Three hundred pounds! Those bison need real groceries!" which confirmed my opinion that just feeding them grass hay was not going to bring Billy, or even The Girls, back to health quickly enough. He advised me to immediately add grains for a heavier diet. He also mentioned that in addition to parasites, they could be suffering from copper deficiency. He added as all doctors tell you, "Consult your own physician." But because Dr. Mario was not experienced with bison, I would have to pull the best information together and proceed from there. I was not going to put the animals' lives in jeopardy over physician etiquette. I asked Dr. Mario if copper deficiency could be a problem. He doubted it because his theory was if copper deficiency were a problem, they all would be suffering from it, and Billy was in worse shape than the others. However, I asked him if I could add a salt mineral block in the pasture, and he said that was fine. I advised Gary of everything that I had learned and everything I was doing to help the animals. The lives of someone elses' animals hung in the balance, and I was taking on a heavy responsibility. I did not want there to be any questions or doubt that I was providing the best of care, should things not work out.

I began to add sweet cob (which is short for Corn, Oats and Barley sweetened with molasses) and various grains and hays to supplement the animals' diet, which pleased them all. . . especially Billy. He was happy to have the sweet cobb fed to him in his special plate, obediently held for him by his Auntie. I also noticed that when I added the three-grain hay to their diet, Billy didn't like the stems, which his instincts told him had no nutrition. So his Auntie cut the stems off for him and gave him only the best part. Billy's ongoing training of me was very successful, with me being an eager learner.

It must have been a cartoonish scene to watch me feed the animals. I literally ran from kid to kid with six different kinds of food, making sure they all had enough. Hand feeding Billy slowed things down, which forced me to run to the others even faster, but I loved every mouthful of it.

Napini continued to make mealtime a real challenge by bullying everyone, especially Whiskey, and making sure no one got more of anything than she did. It was about this time that she started bullying me....mock charging me at the fence. She got a real thrill out of hearing me scream when she lunged at me without any warning. She tried it once with my husband, Robert, but he immediately raised his voice and kicked violently toward her. She backed off and never tried that again. However, Robert had an advantage that I lacked. Napini's taste ran toward good-looking men. Between Billy and Robert at dinner time, she was surrounded by tantalizing virility. She gave Robert plenty of slack, but with me, it was obvious she did not appreciate my love and attention for her buffalo man or her human crush. She let me know it every chance she got with her mock charges. They were mock charges because she could easily have gone through that flimsy fence had she wanted to. The danger was not knowing when a jealous bison female might decide to turn a "mock" charge into the real thing.

Napini was full of contradictions, and my presence added to them. She did not totally trust me near her, yet she completely trusted me with her baby. Some days she wanted to eat out of my hand and let me pat her on the face. On other days she wanted nothing to do with me. Sometimes she would see me and trot happily toward me. Other times, she would be sullen and hang back, looking at me with wild, unfriendly eyes. She could act like a spoiled diva one minute, and then cower away the next. Ultimately, her unpredictability reached the point where it was too dangerous for me to hand feed her, as she sometimes had allowed me to do in the beginning. But she would look at Robert with big, flirty brown eyes and accept his feeding hand with abandon. In fact with such abandon that he had to be careful she didn't swallow his hand with her exuberant style of eating. That girl was complicated and a real handful.

Watching Billy handle Napini was fascinating and a real lesson in love and patience. He wisely gave her a long rope, which she sometimes would take for granted at her own peril. A mate with lesser patience would have been far less tolerant of her pushiness. Billy let her be who she was, but when she went too far, he could generally rein her in with a stern head-butt, or he would simply walk away from her. Napini did not like to be too far away from Billy, and so she would usually defer to him when he let his feelings be known. He seemed to pick his battles with her carefully. She always let him lead the way, and until he made a move, she would stay put. They had a respectful and loving relationship that was touching to watch and made me think how human couples could learn valuable marital lessons by observing the interaction of this buffalo couple.

A week after the deworming, Dr. Mario was right. The diarrhea plaguing The Girls and Whiskey was gone. Unfortunately, Billy's problem was still there, but it seemed better.

After a couple of weeks serving cafeteria-style meals, the animals appeared to be gaining some weight, and I was hopeful that Billy was on the road to recovery. They were all much more excited about their dinner now, with the gourmet style menu and the sweet cob for dessert. As for me, the meal time relay was my new aerobic workout. When the temperature climbed on some days to over 100 degrees, I nearly passed out.

One day I was working in my Bay Area office in Danville, and Robert was in Grass Valley, feeding The Kids. It was the first time he had fed them by himself, and I was anticipating a call, knowing exactly what he would say. As expected, my cell phone rang, and Robert began in a choppy out of breath voice, "I don't know how you do it. How do you do this by yourself?" I heard Whiskey screeching in the background, demanding his share of dinner. Robert responded obediently, yet breathlessly, "Gotta go! The natives are restless. I don't know how you do this every day." Before I could say, "Because I love it." he had hung up the phone to finish serving these hungry, demanding barnyard diners.

When I asked Gary's permission to have Dr. Mario visit and treat the animals, I said I would be willing to share in the expense. But when Dr. Mario presented his bill along with written instructions on their feeding requirements, Gary did not make a move. Embarrassed, I took the bill and handed it to Gary, and after a few uncomfortable moments of silence and inaction, I took out my Visa and handed it to Dr. Mario. Gary made no effort or offer to pay any of the bill. I was very disappointed, not to mention agonizingly broke. But looking at Billy standing there so skinny and frail made it all worthwhile. I felt relieved and hopeful that the animals would be on the road to recovery, and Gary would heed Dr. Mario's advice and begin to feed the animals properly. Money, as difficult as it was to come by in those trying days, was not the issue. A promise to a beloved buffalo was everything.

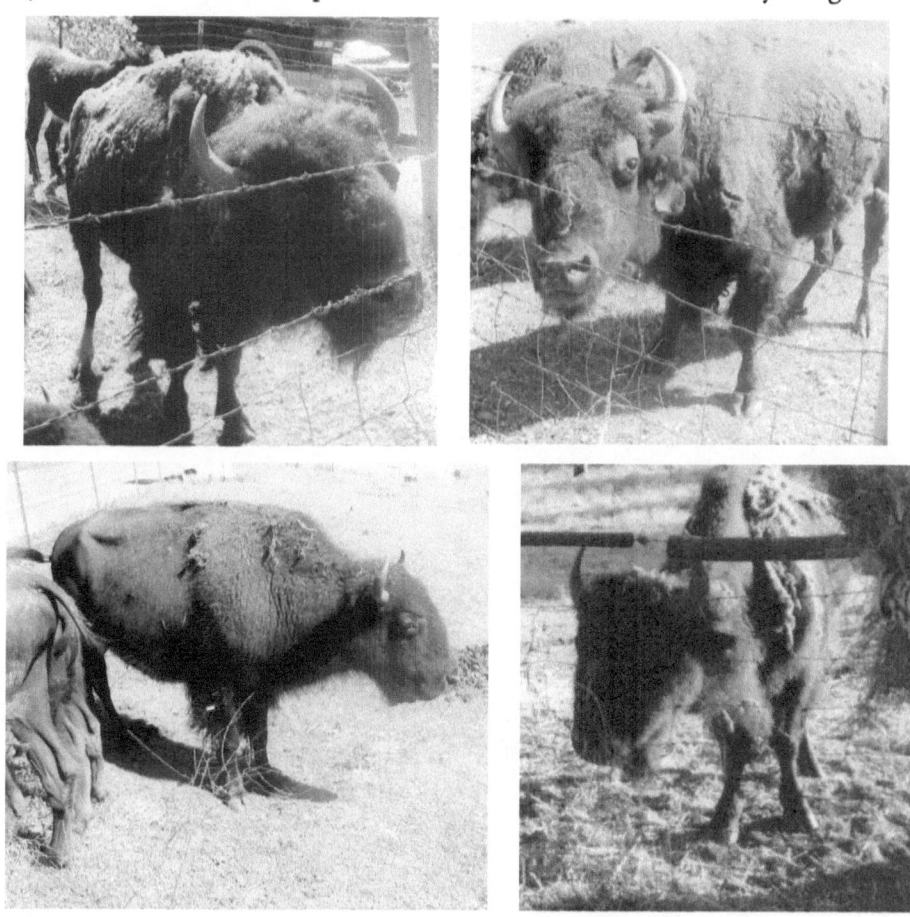

These photos show The Kids when I first met them, looking like walking skeletons.

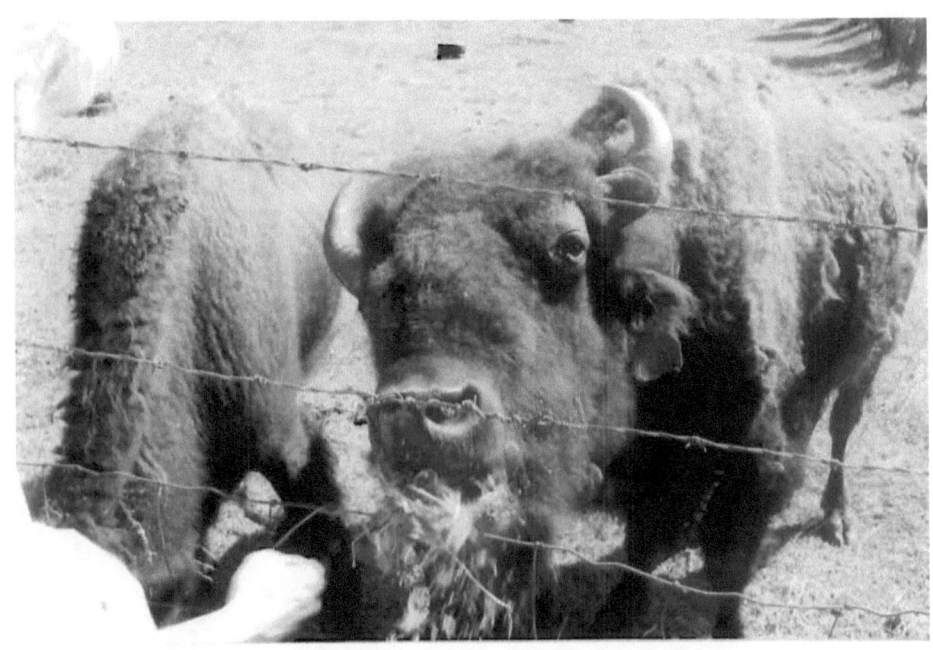

Hand feeding Billy his alfalfa appetizer

Buffalo Happy Hour and Date Night with Billy

Every day that summer with Billy was exciting and rewarding. It reminded me of the anticipation I used to have when I was dating a special guy. I loved the whole preparation of getting ready for a date. What would I wear? How would I fix my hair? What would we do together? Looking forward to something new is one of life's pleasures, and every single day with Billy was a new experience.

Every morning I awoke and thought about him, praying his health would improve. I planned what combination of feed I would bring him for the most nutrition, wondering what new and amazing things he would do or teach me. I could not wait until 4:30 pm....Buffalo Happy Hour.

Since I fed The Kids nearly every day, I learned their habits and preferences, especially concerning food. For example, even though their heads are enormous, they are grazers, and so their mouths do not hold a lot of bulk. I would slice the carrots and apples into just the right size to fit into Billy's adorable square mouth which contained perfectly straight white teeth. Those beautiful teeth were good enough for any advertisement for a Hollywood orthodontist. If the pieces were too big, they would fall on the ground and be covered with dirt. I also cut off the green, moldy carrot tops, and the apples were cored with the bitter seeds removed. I would sit almost every afternoon and happily prepare these buffalo appetizers.

Before the appetizers were placed into bags, I would go to my closet and select an outfit for my date night with Billy. My bison couture consisted of a long sleeved shirt and long pants, not necessarily matching, which served as protection from the barbed wire fence. Then I'd roll up my socks and put on bright pink and green floral rubber boots. You couldn't look at those boots without smiling. No matter what I stepped in, or even if I encountered a snake, I could be happy about it, by simply wearing those crazy "flower power" boots.

My hairdo was usually a ponytail (or in my case a buffalo tail) tucked under an old worn out straw hat, providing protection from the afternoon sun. Then I'd sling a big wet towel around my neck, which kept me cool and provided a way to wipe off my hands. More than once however, this towel shawl created a wardrobe malfunction when it would slide off my shoulders onto the dirt. The wet towel quickly converted the dirt into mud, as I slung it back around my neck. It made a real mess, but while feeding buffalo in the height of a Grass Valley summer, it was much better to feel good than to look good.

Then my "haute look" for the evening would be finished off with a bright colored lipstick, which when I kissed Billy's nose, would leave an unmistakable kiss mark. I doubt if there has ever been another bison that sported bright pink or red lipstick as nose decor.

Raphie, our adorable mutt, who I rescued off the mean streets of Concord, California, was also part of the Buffalo Happy Hour routine. When he would see the carrot and apple bags being carried to the back patio, he would be in the lead...just in case I forgot the way. He would stand and watch the treats being cut, with his tail wagging so enthusiastically that his rear end would sway from side to side. When it was time to load up all the feed, Ralphie would recognize his cue and rush out ahead to supervise packing everything into the car or truck. As I drove off, Ralphie would lie by the front door to await my return after dusk. Buffalo Happy Hour became a ritual we all looked forward to.

I was always careful not to forget to bring Billy's Plate, since he did not want to eat rice bran pellets or sweet cob from off the ground. If I did forget the plate, I would have to feed him out of my hand, which really slowed down the cafeteria style meal service and made the whole gang impatient. An impatient Napini did not create a pleasurable dining experience for any of us.

As for my dates with Billy, while preparation for my long ago dates with men of the two legged variety were not as predictable, I can honestly say that the majority were not nearly as enjoyable.

After I made the arrangements with Gary to feed the animals every afternoon, Robert was usually away during the week so I only had my car to use. If I ran out of food in Gary's barn, I would stuff the feed into my abused car, trunk stuffed to barely closing with orchard hay. Ralphie's mini backseat was filled with trash bags full of sweet cob and rice bran pellets, and the passenger floorboard was crammed with bags of apples and carrots. In the passenger seat was an overstuffed bag of some other variety of hay, which was always encroaching onto my driver's side. The seat was loaded to the ceiling, so when I drove by deer or some other creature on the right hand side of the road, there was no driver to be seen. I learned to drive to Billy's Place stuck up tight against my door for lack of room and to avoid my right arm and leg from being assaulted by the prickly hay. My car radio was tuned to the Christian rock station K-LOVE, and I drove like

Danica along the winding country road. I would sing loudly and mostly off key to inspirational songs like, "He's not finished with me yet" by Brandon Heath and Third Days', "Born again," which spoke to me so clearly. I would thrust my left arm out the window and reach as high as I could, pretending to touch God's hand to shower these precious animals with his blessings through me. That was my driving ritual going to my dates with Billy. Every day was the same, and every day was as exciting as the last.

Billy introducing himself to my Mother. There it is! The "goofy buffalo grin" that I have seen buffalo put on so many faces.

Just Lovin' Billy

I never asked Billy to be anything other than himself, and I never required anything from him. I wanted to honor and protect him. I wanted to know and understand him, and he gave me constant feedback that he wanted the same from me.

The point was not to tame him, which is impossible with bison anyway, and he didn't care about changing me either. He could have easily dominated me; heck, he could have killed me. But because he was as open to me as I was to him, we developed a trusting, caring bond.

Gary and his mother would always tell people that I could get Billy to do anything. I'd chuckle at that because they didn't know that it was mutual. Almost from the beginning of our relationship, Billy knew he had me completely wrapped around his hoof.

I wanted to make Billy's life wonderful to perhaps make up for the suffering and deplorable circumstances he endured, and I was always thinking of ways to spoil him. But Billy just wanted things simple. For a girl who never liked anything simple, it was quite an adjustment. Billy taught me the joy and meaning in simple things, like just being together.

Billy thoroughly enjoyed training me to do what he wanted me to do for him, and whatever he chose to teach me was welcomed and appreciated. I could tell stories about Billy all day long, repeat them a million times and never tire of it. The following are some of my favorites:

One day, I tried feeding Napini with Billy's Plate. She had seen me feed Billy with it every day, but she wanted nothing of it. She grabbed it with her teeth and pushed the plate down, spilling all the pellets. She sucked up that rice bran off the ground like a Hoover vacuum. Billy just stared at her in the patient buffalo way and then turned away from his unruly mate. He turned his attention toward his Auntie and waited to be fed properly. He had such good manners, while Nappy had basically all bad manners and a temperament to match. Because of the way he handled that girl, sometimes I thought Billy wasn't a buffalo at all. I thought he must be a saint.

One afternoon, Whiskey ran up to the fence, behind the bus stop hut, and I began feeding him carrots. I didn't see Billy standing on the other side. When I finally noticed him, he looked rather perturbed at having to wait so long for me to feed him. When I finally approached him with carrots in hand, he gave me "The Horn" and a mock charge, to let me know he did not appreciate my rudeness in making him wait. The insult was further heightened by the fact he had been waiting on an ass!

Giving someone or something "The Horn" is the buffalo equivalent of a human giving someone the finger...except that a sharp tipped, foot long horn is a lot more dangerous, even if it is less insulting. To properly give "The Horn," a bison turns his head to the side and slightly down, and then quickly pulls up his head, leading with his horn. They do this movement usually while stationary. A mock charge, however, is more serious than a Horn finger. "The Horn" is a warning that means, "I am not happy with you." A mock charge is much more serious in announcing, "Now I am really angry and I'm going to show you who's boss." A mock charge is the lifting of both front feet while jolting forward. It is very intimidating because you don't know if it is a mock charge or the real thing coming for you. While the mock charge is a final warning, the real thing is like having a 1500 lb. freight train ramming into you, with the added enhancement and probability of being gored to death.

After Billy clearly showed me that I had been rude to him, I said, "I'm sorry, Honey. Don't be mad at your Auntie. I love you, Honey, don't be mad." I walked up to him again, telling him I wouldn't do anything on purpose to upset him and stretched out my hand with a conciliatory carrot, which he gently took. As he enjoyed his carrot, I patted him on the face, promising to exhibit better manners toward him in the future. I had learned my lesson, and all was forgiven. Buffalo do not bother holding grudges.

When I would visit the herds in Yellowstone, the buffalo would constantly be jabbering to each other. I would constantly talk to Billy, which must have sounded like a bunch of jabber to him. Usually, after I was finished feeding The Kids, the other three animals would walk back to the barn to get a drink, but Billy would stay with me. I would sit down on the ground next to him, separated by a few strands of barbed wire. I would jabber away, and he appeared to listen to every word. Sometimes he would lie down next to me, and we would ponder things together. That is, I would jabber, he would ponder.

One time, he had walked away from me to poop, and I sat down at the fence waiting for him to finish his duty. I leaned over and put my face between the barbed wire and said, "You are such a good boy. Come back here and see me." He walked over and put his face down in between the wire to touch mine. Although I would never be able to put my arms around him, this face hug was even more special because he had wanted it.

I was filling up the water tub and Billy was standing on the other side of it waiting for fresh water. As I was bending over to clean it out, my hat covered my eyesight for a few seconds. When I looked back up….no Billy. I quickly looked behind the barn wall where Billy was making his way past Whiskey's stall. I had inadvertently left the gate open. Billy had his eye on the gate and if he reached his destination, he would be on the loose. I jumped up and ran past him, hoping not to spook him with my sudden move, as we both approached the open gate. I had no choice but to jump in front of him, between him and freedom, yet I knew that if he were determined to escape, I would be no significant obstacle. I said nervously, "No, Honey. You can't get out. We both would be in real trouble." And I began to close the door that swung in front of him. Billy stopped, and looked at me. I said, "I'm sorry, Sweetie." And locked it shut. Billy had a choice in those few seconds: whether to do some damage to his Auntie in order to experience the freedom beyond that gate, or to do her a favor and stay confined.

I realized how much I had jeopardized both of us by being careless, both in taking my eye off him even for a few seconds and by not securing the gate. Fortunately, Billy made the decision to keep us both safe.

Billy allowed me to touch his face, but he never would let me touch the top of his head or get near those sacred horns. One afternoon, after I had fed him his carrots, I patted his face and without thinking, I reached down and kissed him on the nose. Realizing this unexpected move might not be well received. I quickly pulled back; but he accepted it without hesitation, as if he knew what as kiss meant. After that, I greeted him with a nose kiss nearly every day, and he would hold his head up to receive it. I suspected that I was the only person who selected specific shades of lipstick based on how they would standout against the dark brown color of a bison's nose. The ladies at the local cosmetic counter had a lot of fun helping me with the unusual choice of lipstick selections.

Billy and I would be standing next to each other at the fence when he would feel the call of nature. He would walk away from me at least twenty-five ft. and relieve himself. He would never pee or poop next to me. How did Billy know that would be something I would not like? He peed and pooped next to Napini and Minko without hesitation, and even domesticated animals relieve themselves next to their owners. As a child, my best-behaved Shetland Sheepdog once relieved himself on my grandmother's leg to everyone's horror, and moments later, amusement. But a wild animal intentionally holding back from relieving himself until he could walk away from you and do it, was beyond comprehension. That is, if you didn't know my Billy.

I was feeding Billy his carrots as usual and wasn't paying close attention. He gently took a carrot from my hand as he always did. However, I didn't have it positioned in my hand correctly, and my fingers ended up in his mouth. I panicked waiting for a painful bite. He knew that he had my fingers, probably because they did not taste very good, and he stopped chewing. He looked directly and deliberately into my eyes to acknowledge that he had them. Then he took his tongue and pushed my fingers to the side of his mouth so I could retrieve them. Then he resumed eating his carrot. I was so amazed that he did that, but he didn't think it was any big deal. It was just the natural thing to do, to look out for your Auntie.

When I walked along the fence at the street, Billy would usually walk along with me. One time a truck pulled up alongside us and the driver yelled, "That's a pretty big dog you've got there. Nobody is going to mess with you."

I said, "I know and I am the luckiest person in the world." We both laughed and he drove off waving, with that familiar, goofy grin that I have seen buffalo put on so many faces.

While I loved people to stop along the fence to meet Billy, it also infringed upon "our time." Billy did not particularly appreciate that aspect of admirers, and if I spent too much time talking to them, he would make it clear that he wanted me to pay attention to him. He was completely secure without any ego problems to feed, so he didn't require a lot of fan worship. If he felt I had spent too much time with his admirers however, he would give me quite the attitude when they left.

Sometimes his training of me didn't go as well as he had planned, and he would have to resort to The Horn. I would apologize, talk to him sweetly, and he would warm right up again. Eventually, he taught me that I could talk to people who came to see him, if I stood close by and kept eye contact with him. Then he enjoyed his admirers. While I was in training, it must have been frustrating for Billy when it took me a while to catch on.

Often after Billy had eaten his dinner, I'd be sitting on the ground with him lying next to me. As I talked softly and lovingly to him, his eyelids would get heavy, and he would fall off to sleep. I loved sitting there with him so close to me in the stillness of the early evening, listening to the sound of a buffalo snoring. I would sit perfectly still so I could take in every precious moment of it. I had become just one of the herd. He had given me his trust. I had given him my all.

I think Billy was more sensitive to me in his wildness than I was to him in my human ignorance. He was so much wiser about things than I was. How did he know all of these things? Did he reason them in his big mighty head, or did he just know it in his heart? Did instinct and nature whisper to him, or did God himself show him the way? Those sweet brown eyes of his, always observing, always seeking me out, were showing me that I could always understand more if I'd just listen.

My Love Affair with Buffalo Billy

Nature's Gift

Nature is full of mystery and awe. Nature makes us ask questions that will never be answered. That is why I believe we are drawn to her and to all her creatures, plants, and the landscape she rules.

Nature forces us to put things in perspective. We aren't, in fact, the center of the universe. Nature and her domain don't care if we are kings or nameless descamisados; she treats us all the same.

She shows her wonders that can't be found, made, or seen anywhere other than precisely where she wants them, and while unique, are both priceless yet free to all of us. She tells her creatures just what to do and exactly how to do it, and she accomplishes things that are amazingly impossible on an hourly basis. In nature there is no lying, treachery, cheating, hate or envy to muddy things up.

We emulate nature in our quest for dominance, hierarchy and survival, but unlike us, nature has no ulterior motives. There is tremendous peace and comfort when we are in her presence, because it is then that we surrender to the special moments of simple truth and pure existence.

I was in the privileged presence of one of nature's most incredible trophies…the American Bison. I never tired of watching them, interacting with them, and giving them what little I could. I was an outsider to the buffalo. They knew I could never fully understand their world, but they accepted me and allowed me to be who I really am. They gave me the beautiful gift of me.

My Love Affair with Buffalo Billy

The Admirers At The Fence & Jack Arnold

I met so many people while feeding the buffalo at the fence along the street. They would slow down their vehicles and stare in awe at the buffalo or pull over to watch them. Many even got out of their cars to come see them up close and find out more about them. People are drawn to and fascinated by buffalo. Most, I learned sadly, had never actually seen one. Those who had, usually said they had seen the great bison herds in Yellowstone National Park, and they made quite an impression. People would ask all sorts of questions about them which I would gladly answer, usually until I saw their eyes glaze over, and I knew I had probably answered with an overabundance of enthusiasm and information. So goes the discussions of mothers about their kids or an Auntie about her buffalo. But I didn't have to pull out a wallet photo spread. My kids were standing there in all their natural glory staring right back at the admirers at the fence.

Bison are like that. They are as curious about you as you are about them, only they aren't all that excited over you. Since they aren't particularly afraid of anything, they will size you up until they are bored with you or have something more pressing to do….like go lie down.

Once a lady admirer mentioned she loved buffalo but they smelled bad. I had to refrain from informing her that to them, she probably smelled a lot worse. I tried to hide my irritation at the insult she had just thrown at my darlings, and I calmly told her that buffalo, in fact, do not smell bad. She was quite certain that I was mistaken because she had been next to some bison and she said, "They reeked!" Biting my lip and gritting my teeth, I asked her about the circumstances in which she saw the smelly buffalo. She explained that when she was a child, she had seen about a dozen bison confined to a small pen. A wave of sadness came over me as I pictured those proud beasts struggling to survive in a small, squalid enclosure. How frustrating it must have been as herd animals, not to be able to roam, or graze, or even fend for themselves. I tried to get the nightmare of those pitiful animals out of my mind. I explained to the lady that any creature stuck in a small pen all their lives, walking and lying in their own feces and urine would smell bad. In the natural, bison actually have a distinct smell that is almost sweet. I walked up to the fence and grabbed a piece of Napini's hair that had been sacrificed to the barbed wire fence in an earlier attempt to give me one of her temperamental mock charges. I held the tuft of her curly, wiry bangs up to the lady's nose and said, "smell." To her surprise there was no bad odor, and instead she confirmed that it smelled "very fresh." Another convert.

I thought about a small herd I had seen penned up in a miserable fenced lot on the way to Yellowstone. They were purchased to be a tourist attraction at a small motel. My usual joy at seeing buffalo was overshadowed by seeing their circumstances. That lot in Wyoming, measuring about 50 ft. x 100 ft., during the winter would be a muddy feces and urine slush. There was no way for them to run, what's more roam, and their hay was thrown on top of all that muck…just like it was for Billy and The Kids. To look into the eyes of those buffalo said it all. Their normally expressive eyes were blank and defeated by their unjust life sentences. These once proud beasts, the symbol of our country's strength and independence were reduced to show and tell freaks. What does this say about us as a nation? We ought to be ashamed and there ought to be a law.

Those sad buffalo might just as well have been put into a cage. They were doomed to be sick and die before their time to satisfy some traveler's curiosity to see a real live buffalo from the age of the Wild West.

If we confined our other national icon, the bald eagle, to small wire cages, never cleaned them out and left their food to mold and rot on the filthy bottoms, people would be protesting and writing letters to stop it. Yet too many bison are also at the same whim and mercy of man without any real advocacy. Is it because people don't know? Or they simply don't care? These frustrations were the beginning of my idea for a bison foundation to advocate for them and protect them.

After my new buffalo convert had left Billy's Place, my mind wandered to my friend Roger Brooks who had loved his buffalo, Charlie…although Roger didn't know we were friends yet. Roger would pull a tuft of hair from Charlie's huge head and ask people to smell how sweet it was. I never dared to put my hand on top of my kids' heads, what's more yank out some hair. If I tried that, I knew I would be asking for an admonishment more than The Horn. They would never let me anywhere near their sacred horns. Roger had gone where I never could, and it made me a bit jealous.

It never ceased to amaze me how in awe people were of these wild animals and yet how stupid. People would walk right up to the fence and stick their hands through to pet them. A modern, prehistoric animal as big as a car is not something to pet, especially if they realized a buffalo could pick them up as if they weighed five pounds and drop them on their heads. I could usually stop these fools before they were in danger, but on a couple of occasions I couldn't. Luckily, this petting attempt was tried on Billy, and he would fend off their advances just aggressively enough to let them know that it wasn't polite to pet strangers. If it would have been Napini on the other hand, serious damage could have been inflicted.

What irritated me the most is how these people would be so offended that their gesture was not well received. I asked them to imagine Billy's two hundred pound head greeting them with a powerful nudge that knocked them to the ground. That nudge from a one thousand pound buffalo would be their equivalent to a "pet." Should Billy be offended that they fell down? I felt if people really knew and understood buffalo, they would give them the respect they deserve. It's impossible to judge others, even buffalo, if you do not put yourself in the other person's shoes, or hooves in this case. I watched Billy react to things as he put everything in its proper perspective, and I learned how much better things were when I did the same.

But then one day I met the exact opposite of those kind of fools. I was feeding Billy rice bran pellets from his special plate, when an octogenarian cowboy drove up in his Ford Taurus. A short, stocky, sturdy man wearing a summer cowboy hat, jeans, western shirt, and boots emerged from the car, watching me with steely blue eyes. I was familiar with buffalo sizing me up, but not a real live cowboy. Just like the buffalo, I knew this man had something on his mind but said nothing to reveal his thoughts. I said, "Hi there. Did you come to visit the buffalo?"

He said, "Are you the owner?"

I replied proudly, "No, I am their Auntie!" I introduced Jack Arnold to Billy and his gang. Jack told me he had seen me feeding the animals every day and decided to stop and chat. I happened to also be a Jack Arnold mind reader, and I knew he thought I was some sort of strange creature, hand feeding bison and talking to them. He wanted to meet this crazy woman so he could go back to his cowboy buddies, tell a good story, and have a few hardy belly laughs. Cowboys just love a good story. To Jack and his buds, bison were just livestock and they would not understand my love and commitment to somebody else's animals, or to these "INFERIOR" looking animals, as Jack called them.

Oh boy, "stinky" was one thing, but "INFERIOR?" Those were fightin' words. But as I got to know Jack, I knew where he was coming from, being a rancher all his life. He meant no insult. Jack could not help but tell the truth about everything, even if you didn't ask or even want to know. As we became friends, chatting at the fence with the buffalo, I learned that his wife, Lucy, suffered from Alzheimer's and was living her life in a nursing home, a hollow shell of who she once was. Jack would drive by Billy's Place every day on his way to feed and comfort Lucy. He never missed a day. He was the breed of cowboy who loved his woman deeper than anyone could, and whose promise of "in sickness and in health," sealed with a kiss, was a binding contract. I learned that his daughters rarely visited or even called, that he was diabetic, and lived with chronic pain from back and leg problems. I began to know Lucy too through our many conversations about her, and Jack brought me a picture of her when she was young and beautiful. He still saw her that way, although everyone else could only see her as a pitiful, dying, elderly woman, who was lucky to have such a great love.

Jack and I learned a lot about each other during our frequent visits and we developed quite a bond. I knew he wasn't taking very good care of himself. I reminded him that if he didn't, who would take care of Lucy? I cooked meals for him, and he would pick them up and chat with me and The Kids on his way home. While it might sound like I was doing a nice thing for Jack, it was a calculated bribe. I picked his brain constantly, asking questions about his lifelong experience with livestock, much of it pertaining to Whiskey and the buffalo. On every occasion I learned so much from Jack. He was as wise as any veterinarian, and his knowledge on every subject that he knew was captivating. I don't know how much schooling he actually had, but he was a PHD when it came to life and cow-boying. Jack was willing to share all of his knowledge, many times perplexed that I would want to know. Most of all, I treasured his honesty. To Jack, these buffalo were just inferior bred, cattle-like creatures that ended up on a dinner plate. Initially he did not understand my affection and devotion to The Kids. Yet he did understand because he was experiencing the same heartache caring for Lucy, trying everything to make her well again.

But many ranchers have a different feeling about animals. Jack told me he had once shot some herding dogs who were under performing. I was appalled and told him to stop talking about it, but telling Jack not to tell the truth was futile. I couldn't believe I could have a friend who would shoot a dog. Jack never thought he would have a friend who would kiss a buffalo. Some things we just could not understand about each other, but we put those things aside, and didn't let them get in the way of what was good.

I was also convinced that Jack began to look at Billy differently through my loving eyes. Once we were having a long, heartfelt conversation about

Lucy's deteriorating condition. We suddenly realized it had become dark, and I looked over at the barn to see where The Kids were. They weren't at the barn as usual, bedded down. The buffalo were lying down right next to Jack and I at the fence, quietly and sensitively listening to our heart wrenching conversation. Jack shook his head and said, "I wouldn't have believed it, had I not seen it." That was something Jack would frequently say as he began to know the buffalo. Even a hard-core rancher could be touched by a buffalo and his hard core Auntie.

In the middle of the summer, Jack advised me to walk away from the animals. Billy was not improving and Gary was still not feeding them as directed. Jack was fearful that things would end up badly, and he did not want me to get hurt. I told him I could no more walk away from Billy than he could from Lucy. Knowing they might both be hopeless cases, we looked into each other's wet eyes and heavy hearts and understood why the other could never walk away. Even though there were things we could never understand about each other, the more important things that caused us to respect and admire each other kept us tight. Jack was a treasure from the past and I wasn't about to let him go. I don't think he wanted to either. Besides, he loved my quiche.

One evening Jack stopped to find me in a short fused mood. I was glad to see him so I could vent my ire to someone who could confirm my disdain. I ranted and raved about how the feed store had cheated me and sold me some crummy feed that they passed off as sweet cob. I was furious that there were sunflower seeds in it, and so Billy was not going to get his favorite dessert that night. Sweet cob is the abbreviation of Corn, Oats and Barley, with the "sweet" being molasses. I explained to Jack that I had been swindled and bushwhacked into buying something with sunflower seeds, and I wasn't taking it lying down. I called the store manager and told him, "I may be blonde and driving a convertible, but I am no dummy. I am returning this feed and you are going to make it right. I have sick animals whose health and proper feeding is crucial." The manger could not figure out what feed I had been sold and he apologized profusely. But that did not make the situation any better, because Billy and The Kids would not have their sweet cob. So I asked Jack to look at the mystery feed in my trunk and tell me what it was. Jack bent over to look in the bag and raised his eyebrows. I said, "What is that stuff? I can't believe they thought they could get away with this."

Jack kept his head down, casually put his hand over his mouth, but didn't say anything. I detected he was trying not to laugh. Then he looked at me with a grin and said, "Well now. . . " he hesitated in order to break the news gently, "What you're thinking is sunflower seeds is really the barley, you know, Corn, Oats, Barley. . . .sweet COB."

OOPS.

The dumb blonde started laughing, which allowed Jack to finally release his laughter too. I said, "Well then, I guess it's time to serve up dessert!" I turned to Billy and said, "Well aren't you glad Jack stopped by tonight? Not only do you get dessert after all, but your Auntie does not have to make a fool out of herself tomorrow at the feed store."

Jack and I laughed some more. I said sheepishly and certainly not convincingly, "That DOES look like sunflower seeds."

Jack chuckled and said, "Sure it does. . ." and just when I thought he was sympathetic to my stupidity he added ". . . In the dark!"

As I said, there was a lot for me to learn. Fortunately Billy, The Kids and Jack were patient and forgiving. But then I had sweet cob and meat loaf as incentives.

Balenciaga Quadrille

In the beginning of my relationship with the buffalo, I would pull up in my car, or Robert's truck, and the animals would stand there and stare, trying to evaluate the who, what, how, and why someone was stopping at their fence. Like all bison, their every move, and everything that moved around them, was carefully analyzed before any action was taken on their part. The bison's eyesight is not that sharp, and just as they all look alike to most of us, I am sure people all look alike to them. I would get out of my vehicle and call out to them, but because my voice was not yet familiar and I looked like every other human, they were hesitant to move.

However, bison have a keen sense of smell, which gave me an idea to help them distinguish me from other humans who stopped to admire them. If I had a distinct smell, they would be able to recognize me from a distance much farther than their eyes could see. Rather than insult their senses with my Mitchum-masked perspiration, I decided to let them experience the foreign and luscious smell of a designer perfume, whose fragrance would identify me.

When I was about nine years old, my favorite Aunt and Uncle, who frequently traveled to Europe, returned home from a trip to Spain. They brought an admiring and impressionable young niece a small bottle of perfume. One would think that you'd bring a nine year old a gift of cologne rather than the far more expensive perfume. But to my Aunt and Uncle, anything but the best was not in the realm of gift giving possibilities. This wondrous gift had the captivating and exotic name of Balenciaga Quadrille. The perfume bottle had a uniquely designed dome top, and the glass bottle itself was artfully ribbed in a smooth, sleek pattern. I loved the design and feel of the bottle as much as the heavenly scent inside. I used the perfume sparingly, only for special occasions, and it lasted for many years, never losing its original fragrance. When I became of age to buy my own quality perfume, I vowed never to wear anything other than Quadrille, in honor of my beloved Aunt and Uncle, who by that time had passed away. When I wore it, I felt that I still had them with me, if only in a fond, scented memory.

Over the years, Quadrille had actually become my "smell" just as the buffalo came to know it. Before I left to feed The Kids, I made certain that I sprayed some on my neck, which was the only part of my body not completely covered up to avoid barbed wire scars and the punishing sun's rays. I soon realized, however, that this odorous identification scheme was elementary stuff to buffalo. Like almost every other idea I had to teach the bison something, they were always one step ahead. They had learned to recognize the distinct sound of our vehicles' engines. Before I drove up to the pasture, and I could even get out of the car or truck to send my delicate scent their way, they had already started walking toward the vehicle. I am sure there were more Ford F-150 trucks riding by Billy's Place on a daily basis than there were flies on a buffalo patty. But somehow they knew the specific sound of Robert's F-150. My Jaguar had an engine that was so quiet and vibration free that you barely knew it was running. But incredibly, the buffalo heard that car coming, and they knew their Auntie was due to arrive momentarily to serve up carrot appetizers and a four course dinner with dessert.

My perfume idea was a flop because the buffalo were much smarter, but I continued to wear it anyway. I wanted to smell nice for Billy, maybe to make up for my decidedly unattractive buffalo tending appearance.

I will never know if Billy even liked Balenciaga Quadrille. However, no matter the cost per ounce of my perfume, I am sure that he far preferred Napini's fresh natural scent to some laboratory concoction. From what I have read about the infamous designer, Cristobel Balenciaga, I don't know if he would have quite understood or appreciated Billy's scent preference, or my choice of his perfume used as a calling card meant for buffalo.

The Ultimate Buffalo Trophy

Buffalo can move even the toughest of seasoned hunters.

Jerry Martin was an old school chum of mine in Phoenix, Arizona, and grew up in a family of die-hard hunters. When he heard that the state owned buffalo herd in northern Arizona needed to be "thinned out", Jerry and his hunting buddies applied for and received the permits to hunt and kill them. Excited about a new trophy and the experience of hunting an animal with which they had no experience, they set out with their rifles to conquer their new opponents. They had no idea how difficult it would be to track buffalo in the mountains. (I would be able to vouch for that fact later on.)

For three days they tracked the buffalo. Jerry said, "We just couldn't find them. We always knew they were there because there was plenty of fresh evidence left on the ground, but they always seemed to know where we were and remained one jump ahead. They were the most intelligent animals we had ever encountered. They were like ghosts . . . just when we thought we were on them, they would completely and silently disappear."

The hunters marveled at how 1000+lb. animals with tough hooves could be so quiet and elusive. Finally, after three days of tracking the herd, the hunters were resting on top of a hill. They began surveying the landscape, and just below them in a large meadow was the herd.

Jerry said, "We all looked down and were so taken aback at how majestic they were. Every one of us just stood there in silence, watching them in awe. We felt as if we were looking back into history."

After watching the herd for a long period of time, the hunters looked at each other and in unspoken agreement, they knew there was no way they could shoot one of those magnificent beasts. They packed up their gear and went home.

That powerful scene, forever etched in their minds, became the ultimate trophy.

My Love Affair with Buffalo Billy

Buffalo Just Know

Buffalo's tastes change day to day just like ours do, and they can be really picky eaters. One day their favorite food would be three-grain hay, the next day it would be alfalfa. Some days they wanted rice bran pellets first thing, as they weren't quite ready for the sweet cob, thank you very much. They would turn up their noses at rye grass, wanting orchard hay instead, and then the next day make you feel like a complete dolt for not feeding them the rye grass first. It was amusing to guess what to offer them and when, but they had no trouble telling you just exactly what they wanted.

Billy had multi-dimensional communication skills. He would turn his head away from food he didn't want, or give me 'The Horn" if I just wasn't listening. Or he would give me the buffalo stare down, as if to say, "Auntie, I am not eating that!" Recognizing my shortcomings of not speaking his language, he would stand there patiently most of the time, until I finally offered him the one thing he wanted from my vehicle smorgasbord.

Giving the animals the proper nutrition was my primary focus, and I chose alfalfa as a key staple. When the body is experiencing starvation, the muscles, which are made from protein, are eventually consumed for energy. The fastest way to build back weight and muscle is to consume protein, and alfalfa would be the best protein source for the buffalo.

Once I made a critical mistake over an alfalfa purchase, and my faux pas was outed by The Kids:

Robert was out of town, and I asked Gary if he would take me in his truck so I could purchase bales of alfalfa. Gary wanted to go to his feed store instead of mine, and since I was along for the ride, I did not object. (I thought it odd however, that no one there knew who he was. Obviously and unfortunately, he did not frequent the place.) The lady behind the counter offered me "a deal" on some alfalfa. I asked her if it was of good quality, and she assured me it was. I had this romantic notion that all ranch people were like my cowboy ancestors: honest, sincere and caring toward their animals. My long departed rancher relatives, who I am confident were watching from above dressed in flowing white robes and Stetsons, must have been shaking their heads as the alfalfa was loaded into the truck.

When we arrived back at Billy's Place, Gary went up to the house, and I began feeding The Kids. I offered pushy Napini some alfalfa and she turned her head. I offered it to all The Kids and they all refused it. I took a closer look at the alfalfa, and instead of big fluffy flakes, it was practically all stems. I had been had. The buffalo knew that the alfalfa lacked nutrition, and they wanted none of it. My momentary anger at being cheated and disappointing The Kids turned to joy when I thought about it further. When I first began caring for them they were starving and would gobble up anything fed to them. I realized that they were definitely on the road to recovery if they were now refusing "inferior" food. I had also spoiled these magnificent animals, who had developed more discriminating palates as a result of their Auntie's care. In the end, I made my rancher folk proud, as I was thereafter careful to examine feed to make sure it was healthy and nutritious before I brought it home for buffalo dinner.

A Good Ol' Fashioned Tongue Lashing

I was walking out of the grocery store pushing a cart loaded with a 25 lb. bag of carrots, when I saw a man standing next to my car, checking it out. I hoped nothing was wrong with my car, or that he wasn't thinking about burglarizing it. If it were the latter, his only prize would be some left over hay and Billy's empty, dry drooled-on plate. I wasn't too concerned about someone stealing the car, unless they were in the market for a way-to-small hay wagon. As I approached closer I said, "Hi, can I help you?"

He said, "Is this your car?"

I said that it was.

As I was opening my trunk he said, "I just wanted to meet the person who could do something like this."

I didn't know what "something like this" meant so I asked.

As I struggled to put the 25 lb. bag of carrots in the trunk, he walked over to me and I thought he might offer to help. Instead he looked in the trunk, grimaced and said, "Oh Jeez!" and he turned his head away looking pained.

I said, "What?"

He began an impassioned, good ol' fashioned tongue lashing: "Lady, THIS is my dream car! THIS is the most beautiful car ever made, especially with the black pearl paint! Of course who would know what paint color it was! I would KILL to have this car, and just look at what you have done to it! It's filthy! Don't you ever wash this car? How could you treat this beautiful car like this? JEEZ! And it looks like you've been hauling feed in here! What? Do you think it's a truck?!"

The poor guy was getting himself all worked up and distraught. I tried to console him, "You know what? This is my dream car too. You are right. I am ashamed of myself that my car looks like this. But actually I just washed it two weeks ago."

He started walking away. He did not want to have anything to do with his dream car abuser. He said, "Yeah right. This car hasn't been cleaned in MONTHS!"

I said, "No really, you see I feed buffalo every day . . . . ."

There was no explanation that would satisfy him, and he walked off in a huff yelling "Buffalo, yeah right. You should be ashamed!"

I did feel ashamed. I looked back at my poor, formerly beautiful car with the reddish brown clay dirt stuck to it and a variety of hay sticking out of everywhere they could find to settle. It was a mess. As my sad looking car and I drove home, with hay swarming around inside and flying out the windows, I hadn't felt that guilty about anything in a long time. And as people passed us, looking over with a grin at the hay flying everywhere, I slid down farther in my seat, pulling my hat down to cover more of my face.

I had hit the pinnacle of my life in embarrassment, slovenliness, and single mindedness . . . . .and perfect joy.

What I didn't do for The Kids.

The Lucky Ones

One afternoon I was feeding the animals and chatting with Jack Arnold at the fence, when a couple stopped, wanting to see the buffalo up close. They asked me questions about them, as everyone did, and it always gave me the opportunity to spread my mission of bison education. I was always in an evangelical mood, looking for more converts.

There had been so many admirers stopping, that I was getting quite proficient at my passionate presentations. Jack had told me that he loved to watch me talk to people about the buffalo. He said, "You light up like a Christmas tree, and you could sell buffalo to the Indians." I hadn't thought about that before, but he was right. A buffalo foundation had crossed my mind, and maybe I could sell buffalo to people who would buy them, just to let them roam. Who wouldn't want to say, "I own a buffalo!" The foundation could care for them in a natural herd environment for their lifetime, where anyone could come to admire them. It was an exciting and big thought that I filed away in the less occupied left pocket of my brain.

After Jack and the new converts left, I grabbed a handful of alfalfa and fed it to Billy, explaining my new idea to save more of his brothers. He stood and pondered it, as he munched on the greens. Then, all of a sudden, he stopped chewing, opened his mouth, and a big green mass of a mucous projectile flew out as he let out a cough. Unfortunately I was standing in the path of what felt like a wet wind tunnel. I was so stunned I didn't move, and then he coughed again. I had bits of alfalfa and slobber stuck on my shirt, my chin, my cheeks, my eyelashes, in my hair, and even in my mouth. I don't know why these kids liked alfalfa because I can verify that it tastes terrible. Billy was staring at me, probably wondering why his food was stuck all over me. If buffalo could laugh, he would have. I did it for both of us.

Just as I had never seen a buffalo cough I had also never seen one yawn. How many people in the world have seen a buffalo cough or yawn?

One morning, Napini and Minko were lying down together at the barn. They saw me drive up, and got up to greet me and get their carrots. As they reached the fence, Napini opened her mouth and yawned! It was so adorable, seeing all those perfectly straight white teeth with that bumpy brown tongue lounging around them. I pulled out my cell camera, so disappointed that I didn't get a picture. But The Girls were standing head to head next to each other looking so attached, so I held up the phone to snap a picture. Just as if one person yawns another will follow, so it must also be with bison. Minko opened her little mouth and out came a yawn. I snapped the picture.

I think I must have the only rare and priceless picture of a buffalo yawning. Well, I did for a time at least. I immediately went home and e-mailed that picture to everyone I knew. The caption read: Consider yourself one of the luckiest people on earth to see a buffalo yawn.

I got more returned e-mails off that picture than I could answer in a day. Baby Minko had become a star.

Minko yawning!

Only Mud for Water

One late sweltering afternoon I arrived at Billy's Place, fed everyone carrots and apple appetizers from my trunk and then headed to the barn for the hay main course. Napini ran ahead toward the water tub. For years an old rusty bathtub had been set out next to the barn for The Kid's water needs. With three big animals and a 400 lb. baby, that tub would need to be filled frequently, especially in the summer. Napini bent down over it and the bathtub swallowed up her entire head. I yelled, "Nappy girl, I'll get you more water." She looked up and her mouth and tongue were covered in mud. There was no water in the tub, just a layer of wet sediment, and she was so thirsty that she was eating it. I was so upset and said, "Nappy don't you worry, I'll get you some water. You poor girl, don't eat the mud." I had never gone in the pasture with the buffalo, mainly out of fear, but also out of respect for Gary's property because he had never suggested that it was acceptable.

In order to turn on the water spigot, I would have to enter the pasture and walk right in front of Napini. Gary had told me that he went into the pasture with them, but I was not prepared to do that. I tried to remain composed as I walked up to Gary's house. I stood in front of the house and yelled up to him, wiping the sweat off my face, "Gary! Gary!" He came out and I said, "Gary, I am sorry to bother you, but The Kids have no water."

He said, "Really? I'll come down and fill up the tub." I thanked him and went back to the barn to bring out the hay and do my buffalo chores. After feeding the animals and visiting with them, Gary was still a no-show. The Kids really needed water but I could not find the courage to walk into the pasture to turn on the faucet. I waited another half hour but still no Gary. I walked back to the house and yelled, "Gary, I'm leaving now. " No one came out. As I walked by the animals waiting at the tub, I felt so awful not to be responding. I could only hope that Gary would come out and give them water.

The next day, the buffalo and Whiskey were standing near the tub. I immediately looked over to inspect it . . . no water. I was furious. I marched up to the house and yelled "Gary!" After a minute or two he came out on his deck with one of his buddies. I said, "Gary, there is no water again. It is critical for Billy right now not to get dehydrated in this heat, and for him to get well he needs fresh water."

Gary said, "I just filled it up about an hour ago." I said, "Well maybe there is a leak because it is empty." He said he would be "right down." It was the same scenario as the day before. I waited, and waited some more, as did four hot and thirsty animals. They would look at the tub and then look over at me, wondering why I was so dense not to get the hint. The five of us just stood there looking at each other, waiting. Finally my concern for them outweighed my fear of being without the safety of a fence. I said to myself, "I can do this. I am their Auntie. They need water and that's it." I walked to the gate and as I opened it I said, "Okay guys, your Auntie is going to take care of you." I nervously walked to the faucet, while we watched each other, and I turned it on. I was within five ft. of Napini with the rest of the gang next to her. I stayed behind the tub, and filled it up. Then I turned off the faucet and walked back to the gate, feeling so guilty that they treated me with such respect and I had let them down the day before. They trusted me, and when I showed that I didn't trust them, it made me feel very small.

The next day was a repeat: no water. I could not understand Gary. He didn't work and his house was a short distance to the barn. All he had to do was walk down and turn on the faucet for a few minutes. I didn't bother to walk up and call him. I headed for the tub and filled it up. I wasn't afraid any longer, just cautious as you must be with wild animals, and I kept my eye on them.

After saying goodbye to Billy at the fence, I immediately drove to consult with Mark at the feed store. As I drove up, I must have looked as grim as I felt, as Mark greeted me differently. I got out of my formerly black hay wagon, that had become a regular at the feed store, and said, "I am so upset. Mark, you've got to help me."

Mark responded concerned, "Sure."

I explained the water problem and asked him if there was some kind of product that would act as an auto-waterer on a spigot. He sounded relieved and said, "That's no problem." He showed me a simple $25 hook up and how to use it.

I called Gary and told him that I had the solution for filling the water tub. Gary said he had bought an auto-waterer several years before, but the buffalo's horns would catch on it and bend it. I said, "Well, let's give this one a try anyway. It would be so much better for you to have it so you don't have to constantly be filling the tub this summer. Maybe it's a different design than what you had before. Is it okay if I have Robert install it for you?" By this time I knew anything that would make life easier for Gary, or if someone else paid for it, or if he was removed of responsibility, he would be all for it. Knowing this made it easier to deal with him, but it didn't make my growing disdain for him any less. I just tried to rationalize it and find excuses for it, explaining that Gary was just overwhelmed at a tough time in his life.

Just as I suspected, he said, "Give it a try", and thanked me. Gary was always full of thank yous, but they sounded so well rehearsed.

Robert installed the apparatus the next day. Naturally the three buffalo had to inspect every inch of it, as well as Robert's installation, to see if it passed their superior inspection standards.

Gary was right. Their horns would catch on it. So Robert reinforced it and bent it back in shape when the buffalo decided to rearrange the design. I left the water trickling so there would be a constant supply of water and was relieved that The Kids would not run out of water again. That is, when Gary didn't turn off the faucet. Why he did that was baffling. Since a well supplied the water and the float kept the water from overflowing the tub, there was no concern for water conservation or the need to turn it off.

Gary was also not feeding the animals. I saw how much hay was in the barn every day since I brought in almost all of it. I was regularly e-mailing him asking him nicely, gently, subtly, to please feed the animals as we had agreed. He'd feed them 5 flakes in the morning and I'd feed them 5 flakes in the evening. The hay was in the barn. All he had to do was give it to them. Since he just wouldn't do it, I began leaving the additional 5 flakes out for them in the evening before I left, making sure they had food in the morning. I would put it along the driveway fence berm, where it was harder to see. I didn't want Gary to use the excuse that he didn't put it out because I fed them enough.

I sat down with the bills and slashed every expense that didn't involve the bare necessities, to ensure The Kids would be well fed and receive the nutrition they needed to regain their health. However, cutting out expenses didn't prove to be a hardship, because what we received from those animals made up for everything else we did without. Watching them improve and gain weight was reward enough.

I devised a plan that I thought would motivate Gary to buy more hay and therefore save us money. I asked Mark, who understood the circumstances, if he would agree to offer Gary a three for two hay deal. If Gary would buy two bales he'd get one free. There would be no way Gary could buy hay any cheaper. Mark would then charge my Visa for the third bale without Gary knowing it. Mark was sympathetic, and he readily agreed. I enthusiastically told Gary about the great hay deal from Mark, thinking he would really appreciate it and take advantage of it. But Gary never took him up on it. He just continued to rely on us. I was so frustrated when I thought about it, so I decided not to think about it. I thought about what was best for the animals.

Five Star Service and Accommodations

I asked Gary if we could clean out, or in rancher lingo, "muck out" The Kids' stall. From our view at the fence, we had never seen Gary muck the stalls or any evidence they had ever been done. Gary responded, "Have at it!"

The experts on buffalo say that they will never go into barns, but then they never asked these buffalo what their preferences were. This family of three went into this 15 ft. x 15 ft. tight stall and slept together.

We had suspected that it was dirty, but when Robert and I looked in, it was nothing but a foot deep of feces mixed with dirt and urine. With the filthy conditions, I was amazed Minko had survived at all. When buffalo babies are first nursing, if feces contaminates their mother's milk, it can be fatal. I also thought it was amazing that they all didn't smell terrible.

Robert and I were determined that these American Icons would have a clean, dry place to sleep, which would be helpful for their recovery. I contacted the organization Animal Welfare Approved (AWA), which has the highest standards for the care of animals. I explained my idea for the optimal bedding: we would first shovel out all the manure, disinfect the floor and walls with a powerful veterinary solution, and after it was dry, we'd apply lime as a first layer to help kill bacteria. We would then add a layer of sawdust to absorb liquids, a layer of straw, another layer of lime and then another of sawdust and straw. We'd have a nice soft bedding of about 18 inches thick. The AWA gave me their approval, Dr. Mario gave me the green light, and so the next afternoon we began our cleanup project. Robert, bless his heart, began shoveling up the ripe, foul mess, and when he was done, it was my turn to apply the disinfectant. Robert then went to look at the bathtub.

Robert shouted to me, "You have got to come see this!" I put down the disinfectant, took off my sweaty face mask and walked over to the tub. The water was almost black with algae and there was a layer of dark green slime floating on the top. The spigot had been turned off. We stared at the tub and then stared at each other with grimaced faces, thinking about these animals having to drink this unhealthy soup. Robert said in disgust, "They have to have clean water!" and he began to drain the tub. As Robert worked furiously at his bathtub duty, I was hoping the buffalo girls didn't hear his language that was as foul as his task.

The bottom of the tub was thick with sediment, which Robert scooped out with his hands. Then he sprayed down the tub as clean as he could. He was really angry; not that he was cleaning out the tub for the animals, but that it had not been cleaned in months, maybe years, maybe ever. Robert scowled, "Tomorrow I will bring a wire brush and get this cleaned up right. Your boy, Billy must have clean water so he will get better. No wonder they all had diarrhea!" After the tub was refilled, Robert went into the barn and Napini came over, tentatively inspecting the mysterious crystal clear beverage. She appeared hesitant to drink it, as if she didn't know what clean water looked or smelled like. But soon her thirst took over, and she put her mouth and nose completely into the water and began vacuuming it up with her lips. We had never actually watched the buffalo drink. We assumed she would lap it up with her tongue like Ralphie. However, nature always has a better way and a reason for everything. What could be better than this method, which would keep the buffalo's mouth and nose clean? Just when you think you know it all, nature shows you that you aren't that smart, and how much better things are when you weren't involved in the design.

Robert and I then went back to the stall, to prepare the bedding. Bison are intensely curious and want to know and figure out everything that is happening around them. And no buffalo was as curious or as much of a control freak as Napini. As we were working on her new bedroom decor, one of us had to keep an eye on her. We didn't know how she was going to react to us being in her private space, and if she wasn't happy and decided to run in after us, we wanted to have enough warning to jump into the next stall for protection. Nappy stood about 20 ft. away and watched our every move, trying to figure out what we were doing to her bedroom. As Robert and I worked feverishly adding layers of lime, sawdust and straw, she seemed amused at her new domestic help. Finally, we were done and stepped up into the next stall and closed the gate, to wait for her inspection. She walked in slowly, looked all around the room, sniffed the bedding, and proceeded to pee. Then Minko came around the corner to see what her mom was doing. She walked around on the cushy bedding and then she peed too. Then they both walked back outside, because it wasn't their usual bedtime. Robert and I both chuckled at their same response. I rushed back into the stall, pitched the wet areas, added lime, and refreshed the straw for Billy. Pretty soon, he also came in to check out the redecorating job. I said, "Come on in, Honey, and see how nice it is. Now when you lie down and get up, it will be a nice comfy carpet for your shins." Billy was looking intently at the bedding, and while walking luxuriously on it, he proceeded to poop. I said, "Well I guess that means you approve? But the point is for you to have nice clean bedding, so can you try not to do that again?" Robert and I laughed and shook our heads, but the joy and satisfaction that we felt for their new, clean, comfort was undaunted. After Billy left the stall, I ran back in to pitch the poop and fluff up his new bed.

The next day Robert and I could not wait to see if the bedding was a success. The trio now had five star accommodations and turndown service. We expected they would leave us a tip now and then, and we weren't disappointed. The Kids had definitely slept there, because along with the indented outlines of their bodies in the straw, there was one little girl poop left as proof.

Thereafter, the daily routine was cleaning out their stall and tub, while Nappy stood supervising "The Help." With the bedding system in place, cleaning out any residue was quick and easy and it stayed fresh and clean. We couldn't believe how easy it was to maintain.

Sometimes we would stay later in the evening until the family was ready to bed down, and we would watch them lying down together on their clean, soft bedding. I don't know who enjoyed it more, us or the buffalo.

We had moved a few bales of straw into the barn in order to be able to refresh the bedding. One afternoon we arrived to feed The Kids and as we walked to the barn we noticed some of the straw lying in the covered area where Gary would throw out their food. Robert and I looked at each other for a few minutes, and he said, "You tell him." Gary spotted us doing our chores and came down from the house to chat. I had been rehearsing what I was going to say to be kind and not sound threatening in any way.

We all said our hellos along with a few minutes of small talk, which always included me telling him about something fun or interesting that his animals had done that day. I summoned my diplomatic posturing and said, "Gary, I noticed there is straw under the metal cover."

He said, " Yeah, but they don't want to eat it. I guess they'll eat it when they get hungry enough."

I said, "Well actually that is just straw. It's what we brought for their bedding and they probably won't eat it. It has no nutritional value, kind of like us eating cardboard." Then I quickly changed the subject to talk about something Billy had done that was amusing, and nothing was said again. It made me wonder if Gary had fed The Kids straw in the past, not knowing what it was and because it was a lot cheaper than hay. I guess starving people will eat cardboard too, if that's all there is to fill an aching empty stomach.

One evening after we had concluded our maid service at the barn, Billy walked in to inspect. I was watching him from the gate of the next stall, and from there, our heads were at the same height. He looked so enormous from that vantage point. After his brief inspection, he walked over and startled me with a complete face wash with his giant tongue. (Gene Simmons, eat your heart out!) Billy had never licked me so lusciously before, and never on my face. . . from my chin to my forehead. I quickly wiped the drool off of my lips and my bangs. Robert and I were laughing, but Billy just stood there looking at me and didn't walk away. I thanked him for the beautiful kiss, put his face in my hands and kissed him on the nose. I hoped he wasn't disappointed that my affection wasn't returned as slurpy as his. Then he turned around to lie down for the night, as The Girls came in to join him.

I said what I always said in leaving for the night, "Good night, Billy. I love you. See you tomorrow. Good night, girls. Love you too." Sometimes I felt them saying "Good night" right back.

On another balmy evening, after I had jabbered lovingly to Billy from the adjacent stall and kissed him good night, he walked around his stall, and picked just the right spot to lie down. Ever vigilant Napini had been waiting outside the barn watching us. She walked over to Billy and lowered her head within inches of his. He didn't flinch and she began nuzzling the top of his head with the top of her head, which she could only do if he were lying down. I had never seen a gentle move of any kind from Napini, even with her baby, Minko. But there in that stall, she nuzzled Billy's head again, moving gently back and forth. She stopped to look into his eyes and began again. He held his head up to receive her adulation. After a few moments, she stopped, walked a few feet away, and looked over at me. I felt she was showing me that no matter what I did in human terms, there were some things only a buffalo could do exactly right. I chuckled and gave her that. I wanted Billy to have all the love there was, but I was a little jealous that she had permission to touch his thick, curly bangs and his magnificent horns. Her loving gesture had put me in my place. My love for Billy had to be shown in foreign ways that he grew to accept and understand.

I walked away from my darling boy resting in the comfort of the barn, surrounded by Nappy and Minko, all cozied up together in that stall.

There was no doubt that Billy would go to sleep that night feeling loved, protected, and cherished by all three of his girls. I felt such a rush of quiet peace.

I walked out of the barn into the last moments of the sunset. There was a stillness that seemed like time had stopped. I looked up at the faint remnants of the red sky that the sun had tossed over the horizon of 60 foot pines. The jagged edges of those silhouetted tree tops, along with the loveliest color of soft twilight I had ever seen, seemed like one of those moments when you aren't sure you are seeing something real. My entire body was at peace from being so close, so personal with God and nature, who had revealed themselves to me in my love for a buffalo. I did not want that moment to end. I walked slowly back to my car, with my eyes focused on the fading horizon. I wanted to grasp every second of it, trying hard to make it last, knowing any effort on my part was useless against time.

In a few moments darkness silently overtook the red haze, but replaced it with the crisp twinkling light of the stars that can be seen this way only in the clean, clear air of the mountains. As I got in my car, I looked back at the barn, picturing those beautiful animals lying together in contentment. I smiled, and that movement of my face broke the spell. I was back to reality, and as I looked up at the stars, I always wanted to remember that feeling and that moment. No matter what lay ahead, I would never forget those fleeting moments of perfect peace

My Love Affair with Buffalo Billy

Time To Meet My Friend Roger Brooks

I had been introduced to Roger Brooks through the entertaining book, A *Buffalo in the House.* The author, RD Rosen, described Roger so succinctly in his book that I felt I really knew the man. I had held off contacting Roger after I read the book, but at the time I did not exactly know why.

Now I knew. Now I could contact him, not as someone with whom I lived a vicarious dream of having a bonded relationship with a buffalo as Roger had with Charlie, but as someone who also lived that dream. How many people in America could really understand my experience with Billy? How many people on the entire continent had actually touched a buffalo, stood right next to one without fear, and hand fed one carrots? How many people on the planet had kissed an American Bison or had one kiss them enthusiastically right back? How many lucky people in the universe had fallen in love with a buffalo and had been loved by one just the same?

Roger and I belonged to a rare and special club, with very few members who could share our mutual experiences. There were bison experts out there, experienced ranchers and brilliant and caring vets and professors like Dr. Woodbury, but they did not know bison in the way Roger and I did.

I am sure most people thought of Roger and me as stupid, or careless, or just plain crazy, to put ourselves so up close and personal with a bison. However, Roger and I knew we were thoughtful people, trusting but still cautious of a wild animal, and yes, we were crazy. . . crazy in love. But whatever we gave to our buffalo, and it was everything we could, we got so much more from them. If we were considered crazy for being completely happy in a state of grace and peace because of our love for Charlie and Billy, then we would plead insanely guilty. Roger and I feel so much gratitude for our buffalo pals, and we feel so sorry for the rest of the world for not having had the joy of such a truly unique and special friend. If everyone knew buffalo as we do, not one would be slaughtered and they all would be protected.

Animals are like humans in that they all have their own personalities. Many people don't recognize that they have feelings, a definite thought process, and have different communication skills among themselves versus interacting with humans....in a way being bilingual. However, there are millions of people who love whatever type of animal they own, and they completely understand how much animals are capable of. Bison are no exception. Roger and I were just fortunate enough to have known two special bison boys who had the desire to have a human relationship and took it as far as they did, with us being eager to accept it and learn all we could from it.

It should always be up to the animal to decide what that relationship will be with a human; we can't force it. We can sometimes train them to do what we want, but we can't make them be what we want. Just as you can't change a person's personality and genetic makeup, it's the same with animals.

From reading the book, I knew that Roger was a man of few words, but there was so much I wanted to tell him, so much I wanted to share with him about Charlie and Billy. But I knew that I had to contain myself and start out slowly. My friend, Tina Parkman, had sent Roger a very friendly and lengthy e-mail after she read his book. I chuckled when I read it and thought, Roger is going to respond with one brief sentence. And so he did.

I did not want a one sentence response from Roger. I wanted a friendship because of what we both shared. I wanted a relationship, even if it was just through an occasional e-mail. So I carefully worded Roger's first introduction to me and Billy. He and I had a lot in common. He attended Arizona State University and I was a Sun Devil too. I had my private pilot's license, and he was also a pilot, but he had far more experience as a fighter pilot, having served in Vietnam. He and I took on the extraordinary care of two sickly male buffalo, and we would surely love and understand each other for it.

But we were also different. Roger was the strong silent type, I am a jabberer. He revealed that he had never read the book about him and Charlie. I not only read it several times, gave it to as many people as I could, but I would be writing my own story. Roger raised Charlie from a two week old baby; I had met Billy as a full grown bison.

I have to admit I was envious of Roger, for having those precious growing up years with Charlie that I had missed with Billy. Yet because of that, I also felt I had something even more special. Roger had raised Charlie from an infant, and as far as Charlie was concerned, Roger was his real dad, who also became his buddy. It was natural that they would have their special bond. But I met Billy when he was six years old. We bonded within a few weeks in the same strong and loving way. That made Billy an extraordinary animal, and to me, even more special.

I also met Minko as a baby but she had both buffalo parents to love and guide her, unlike Charlie who was an orphan. Yet Minko was like her Daddy and opened her heart to a special relationship with me that would remain a part of her.

I felt elated when Roger responded to my introductory e-mail with an actual paragraph. And after that, we communicated frequently. Roger gave me advice, his support, and his friendship, which I was eager to receive and return. His kindness came through in his e-mails, but most of all, his undying love for his Charlie. I completely understood.

My Love Affair with Buffalo Billy

Buffalo Heroes, Ted Turner and Mike Mease

Today there are approx. 200,000 bison in the US and approximately 200,000 in Canada, with over 90% living on private ranches that raise them as livestock for meat. Sadly, last year over 60,000 were sent to be slaughtered.

However, there are only about 15,000 bison left in existence that have pure American Bison DNA. There was a rancher at the beginning of the last century, who will remain nameless for his crime, who decided to challenge nature and cross breed cattle and bison. However, nature would have none of it, as bison would never find common cattle romantically appealing. So this rancher artificially forced the cross breeding of the two species and therefore forever tainted the future of the American Bison population.

The last wild, free roaming herd of true DNA bison located in Yellowstone National Park number only around 3500-4000. Thanks to the 15 years of tireless effort by the small but fiercely committed Buffalo Field Campaign, and it's co-founder, Mike Mease, the killing, slaughter and confinement of bison wandering out of the park had been reduced, but sadly not eliminated. For example, during the 2007-2008 season, an astonishing 1613 bison were killed, but in 2009-2010 the number was drastically reduced to 22. However, over the past few years the numbers have been escalating, with the 2014-2015 season reporting 740 of these national treasures killed. That number represents about 20% of the largest and last wild, genetically pure herd in America being eliminated. The reason given for the actions against the bison is the disease, Brucellosis, that ironically bison contracted from cattle. Some of the bison in Yellowstone have tested positive for the disease, which causes cattle to abort. The cattle industry fears that the bison wandering out of Yellowstone will contaminate their cattle, yet the elk in and around Yellowstone also carry the disease and there is no such effort to confine and kill them. Further, there has been no scientific proof that wild bison have ever passed Brucellosis onto cattle.

A hundred and fifty years after the Great Bison Slaughter, our government is still systematically killing off, hazing, and confining these national treasures and spending over $1,000,000 a year to accomplish it. Those buffalo in Yellowstone are descendants of our country's history that belong to all of us. They belong to the ages.

To put it in further perspective, there was an article recently announcing that maned wolf pups were born in captivity at the Smithsonian Conservation Biology Institute. The birth of the cubs, which are on the "Near Endangered Species" list was revered and highly prized because there are only about 20,000 maned wolves left in the wild.

The Smithsonian is spending all this effort and resources on a South American wolf, when our own American icon, who is also on the "Near Endangered Species" list, has been reduced to only 3500 left in the wild. Yet our government is actively engaged in killing or confining these last 3500 American Icons.

Thanks to Ted Turner's love of the buffalo and to the tremendous resources he has committed to their future, there are approximately 55,000 bison who roam on thousands of acres on his privately owned ranches.

In 2010, eighty-eight Yellowstone bison, who were confined and quarantined during four long years of Brucellosis testing, were able to be released. Our government refused to allow them back into Yellowstone, but no one including Native Americans, would step up to take them. Thankfully, Ted Turner had the heart and the resources to spare these innocent animals that were headed for slaughter. He took them to one of his ranches, thereby insuring their rare DNA would live on.

He has deeded his vast landholdings into conservation easements for permanent open space. I had the privilege of thanking Ted personally for his heartfelt generosity, that at least on his land, bison will forever roam. Years later, under the original agreement with the government, Ted released most of the Yellowstone bison he had saved to a Native American tribe.

Contact the Buffalo Field Campaign for more information on the plight of the Yellowstone Bison and the Brucellosis controversy. Tell Mike that Billy's Auntie sent you.

www.BuffaloFieldCampaign.org

Never a Fence Between Us

One Friday afternoon, Robert was engrossed in his bathtub scrubbing duty, and I was standing at the fence along the street with Billy. The Girls had finished their dinner and were walking back to the barn to get a drink. They were approaching Robert at the tub, and he did not see them coming. I yelled to warn him but he could not hear me. I continued trying to warn him, concerned they would come up next to him without the protection we had always had of the fence. I was screaming and waving my arms but to no avail. Finally Minko walked up directly behind him, with her mom about six ft. behind her, and nudged his back pocket that contained a cache of carrots. Startled, Robert quickly turned around to find Minko looking up at him expecting those carrots, with Napini passing Minko and walking directly up to him too. I held my breath. I saw Robert's face turn somber and he looked over at Billy and me to see if we were observing this unsettling situation, perhaps looking for guidance we could not give. He turned to Minko and took the carrots out of his pocket to feed her. Napini took one more step closer to get her treat, which Robert very promptly gave her. The Girls stood munching on their carrots, relaxed and happy. By this time, Robert's mouth had been gaping open with a fearful, yet huge grin. His eyes were open so wide that his eyebrows had jumped almost up to his forehead hairline. The Girls held their heads out for more carrots and he quickly obliged. I felt as frightened yet as excited as was Robert. When all of the pocket carrots were eaten, The Girls casually turned away from him and walked in front of the tub to get a drink.

Robert tried but failed to walk back to the barn as casually as they had walked away from him. Once in Whiskey's stall where The Girls could not see him, he looked over at Billy and me and began waving his arms and jumping from side to side in pure elation. His face sported such a wide grin I thought his cheek muscles might freeze up. Both of us were laughing nervously from the excitement of what had just happened. Neither of us had been that close to the buffalo without the security we felt with the fence as a separation.

It was obvious that the buffalo had known all along what we also knew: that flimsy fence had been no real obstacle between us had they wanted to breach it. While we chose to pretend that three strands of barbed wire and some wire mesh below it was a protective barrier, the buffalo were a lot wiser, not finding the need to pretend or consider it so. To them, we had been standing right next to each other at dinner time since day one; therefore, it was perfectly normal to walk up and stand next to Robert in the pasture and ask for some carrots.

The buffalo had not considered the fence to be any kind of protection for us, and why would we need protection from them? It was as if in human terms, we would be standing next to a ribbon held taut with one of our friends on the other side. We would not have considered that thin piece of fabric any kind of protective obstacle either, and why should our friends be afraid of us?

Buffalo will not normally approach people, and in most cases, will stay away and turn away if approached. Neither Minko nor Napini would get anywhere near strangers or even Gary, yet they had been standing next to me on a daily basis and next to Robert when he was present. By The Girls casually walking up to Robert for treats, we realized how much they had trusted and accepted us and how clueless we were compared to the minds and understanding of these buffalo. We were reminded of this time and again in various circumstances, which always made us feel small, ungifted, undeserving, and even ignorant.

Robert commented on how much bigger and more powerful Napini had felt standing next to him in the open and how much smaller he had felt, even at 6' 2" and 210 lbs. However, she had not changed nor had he. It was the perception of being in control, or being safe even with an inadequate fence, that falsely made Napini seem less powerful and more manageable.

When we realized how they had felt about standing next to us at the fence, we felt ignorant and embarrassed at our lack of understanding. However, this encounter with Robert made us feel incredibly special because they felt being close to us was so natural. It was even more amazing that a bison mother would allow her baby to accept us so freely. We had become part of their family and until then, we did not fully understand it or truly appreciate it.

The buffalo had again put us in our place, while at the same time, made us feel very important and uniquely fortunate.

Buffalo Speak

Buffalo have fascinating and quirky communication skills. We will never know what their grunt speak means, but clear messages are broadcast from their tails. If they are relaxed and content, their tails are hanging limp and are free swinging. If they are becoming agitated, their tails begin to rise. This signal gives everything and everyone time to straighten up or get the heck out of the way. If they are really upset, their tail position is straight up, but by that time, whatever is in their path will risk being seriously wounded or find themselves dead from the charge. Imagine being hit by a BMW SUV at 30 miles an hour with two sharp sticks as protruding hood ornaments. That pretty much sums up why healthy adult bison have no predators. It is awesome to see two male buffalo charging each other head on during the rut, or mating season. With their thick skulls and dense hair cushioned heads, nature has provided the only way they could survive the blows. No other animal could.

When I was feeding Napini and Billy, it was sometimes difficult to see over their heads to see what their tails were saying, so I always tried to stand a bit to the side to be able to determine what they were thinking.

On one occasion, the bison were feeding casually at the fence, when suddenly Billy, and then Napini, stepped back, tails raised high. They appeared to be looking up the hill behind me. I stepped out of their way, never turning my back-to them, knowing that fence was no match for charging bison. I looked behind me but couldn't spot anything unusual, and I looked back at the buffalo to follow their line of sight. They stood perfectly still and tense, tails raised, eyes glaring. Bison can smell trouble from three miles away while our eyes can only scan the immediate landscape. I began to scour the hill more closely, and I finally spotted a very large coyote about a half mile away. I would have sworn it was a wolf but none have ever been seen in our area. With its light brown coat it was difficult to see in the tall brush, but the buffalo had caught the scent and were on high alert. Napini and Billy hated the neighbor's dogs, relating them to predators, but they had never acted on such high alert with the dogs. Nature had told them the coyote was a different type of canine, obviously by a distinctly different scent. By this time little Minko's instincts had kicked in, and she retreated to the safety of her dad, but defiantly raised her little tail too. A girl can really act brave in the shadow of her knight in shining armor.

When the threat was gone, long after I was able to see it, the buffalo relaxed and resumed their meal. This encounter was another reminder of our basic inferiority to nature.

In Yellowstone it is exciting to listen to the herds communicate with each other in a deep baritone language that is hard to describe but very distinct. Their "speak" is a combination of a grunt and a soft growl.

Just as with humans, some bison are very chatty and jabber to everyone, and some are quiet and more reserved. Minko was a jabberer. She loved to jabber away at her mom and dad. Billy wasn't a talker, but Napini would occasionally answer her back. Minko didn't mind or feel the least bit slighted. She just loved to hear herself speak.

One afternoon she was saying the most entertaining things to herself and whoever would listen, and she was bobbing her little head in amusement. Evidently Napini wasn't all that amused because she was ignoring her. So Robert felt she deserved some recognition, and he answered her with his best guttural-friendly buffalo impersonation.

Minko stopped, looked over at him as if to say, "He can talk!" and she answered him back. From then on, Robert was hooked on buffalo speak. He would practice in the shower, he would practice with other people (who had no idea what he was saying either) and he became quite fluent in a language that he had no idea what anything he said meant. When he spoke buffalo, Napini would turn and look at him, but she would never respond. Perhaps she was not impressed with his accent, or maybe it was his grammar that was off. Or maybe she didn't' want to give him the satisfaction. However, Minko loved to converse with him. It was so adorable to listen to them talk back and forth, and we hoped that whatever he was saying was encouraging her to be the best, most beautiful, and smartest little buffalo girl. We told her that in English too, recognizing that being bilingual can be a real advantage to a girl nowadays.

The humbling thing about bison communication was that The Kids understood so much of what I said to them and caught on so quickly. I was never able to figure out a word of theirs. I was only smart enough to understand tail language.

Bison also use their horns as communication devices. We were given The Horn more times than we would like to admit, but fortunately the mock charge was not that familiar.

We were able to watch Minko when she first began practicing The

Horn. She held her head up and wiggled it around. No, that wasn't quite right. Then she tried moving her head back and forth, which didn't feel right either, so she tried an around-the-world action. Nope, try again. She held her head down, forgetting to bring it back up and waved her horn around. She was a smart little girl, and after a few weeks she had it down pat. But then she had to learn what it was for. One day she was running to the fence to greet me and decided to show her Auntie that she had mastered the art of The Horn. . . not a good idea to run and do it. She nearly threw herself over. It was so much fun watching her learn how to be a buffalo. She was smart, funny, kind, beautiful, loving, and just plain perfect! Of course, she was Billy's girl.

However, looking into a buffalo's eyes was always my way of figuring them out. Unlike a lot of animals, they have no problem looking you straight in the eye. Their eyes can be piercing, irritable, loving, playful, and thoughtful. Their expression is so easily read, and they will attempt to read yours too. Whoever said the eyes are the entry to the soul must have known buffalo.

My Love Affair with Buffalo Billy

Waking Up On the Wrong Side of the Stall

There was only one time that I ever saw Billy in a bad mood.

On a beautiful day in mid-July I arrived at Billy's Place, but he wasn't interested in eating nor did he want to chat. I had left plenty of food out the day before, so I wasn't concerned that he hadn't eaten. I offered him carrots and apples but he turned his head away. I tempted him with grass hay, and then rye hay, but he refused them both and gave me The Horn. Instead of listening to him tell me he wasn't hungry, I held out some three grain hay, after breaking off the stems he didn't like, but in return he gave me a mock charge.

Billy had never given me a mock charge before, and it was a reminder that I had to be always cautious. Even though Billy was gentle and receptive by nature, wild animals will always be unpredictable.

I said, "Wow, are we in a bad mood today? Okay, I get it. I'll just leave you alone. When you're ready I'll be here. I love you, Honey, even if you are a big grump today."

He did not have that sweet look in his eyes. He didn't look like he was ill, he just looked annoyed. I looked at his tail to see just how annoyed he was. His tail told me he wasn't too upset, but just to be sure, I walked away from him a few feet and put his big plastic plate on the ground filled with the usually irresistible sweet cob. I said, "Here's some dessert if you want it later. Maybe that will sweeten you up." The sweet cob tempting him from his plate did not interest him or move him.

It was common for Napini to be in a bad mood, but this was a first for Billy. Naturally I was disappointed, but I didn't approach him further. He had made it very clear that he had gotten up on the wrong side of the stall that morning, and I couldn't change it. He just wanted to be in a bad mood, and that was that.

Minko and Whiskey were more than happy to be the focus of my time and attention, and Nappy just wanted to enjoy her food in solitude. She had no use for dinner guests. They were only good for getting bigger portions when she could bully them off and finish their share of food too. After everyone was fed but Billy, who was still pouting over something he wasn't revealing, I headed to the barn to do my chores. Minko followed me, happily trotting along beside, like father like daughter. But today Billy stayed put, content in his funk.

However, when it was time to go, Billy was standing at his usual place at the fence by the road waiting to see me off.

I said, "I am sorry you were feeling grumpy today. But it's alright. We all have a bad day now and then. You know I love you no matter what." Even in a snit, he wanted to make sure I was safely off and to watch me disappear down the road as he always did, just as one would do when a good friend leaves after a warm visit.

The next day, I wore some Barbie pink colored florescent lipstick I thought might cheer him up, hoping no one else would see me wearing this ridiculous color. But when I drove up to Billy's Place, things were back to normal. He was waiting at the fence, ready for a lipstick kiss and all the adulation (and sweet cob) a doting Auntie could give.

I discovered why Barbie dolls are always shown with Barbie Pink colored lipstick. After I had kissed Billy with it, it didn't wear off either of us for three days. I wished I would have known that because I would have put it on more carefully. Whatever formula was used in that lipstick should be turned over to the defense department for some kind of long term weapon development.

The Carrot and The Stick

One afternoon I was feeding the animals when Gary approached. He began with some small talk, and then mentioned he was as seriously thinking about selling the animals because it was becoming "too much for him" with all of his other problems. I never thought of the animals as a problem, and since I was essentially taking complete care of them, nothing would change if I bought them except geography. Gary said he knew I loved them, and that he'd like to see me have them. Then Gary dropped the bomb. He said that someone else was interested in buying them. He said he would make sure that whoever bought the buffalo would not buy them for meat. Then he made an even stranger comment that he would "shoot them himself, rather than have them be sold for meat." Ironically within a few months he would be threatening to do both.

That was a curious, disturbing statement that made no sense at all. He had complete control over what happened to his animals. He knew I adored Whiskey, and he knew if I owned the buffalo, they would never be slaughtered. After I had loved and tended to those animals with such commitment, why would he even think of selling his animals to someone else?

If his motivation was to get the highest price, it was cruelly effective. Who would pay more than I would, with my emotional attachment? I would have remortgaged the house, taken a loan out on my car, and perhaps even on Ralphie. I did not know what to think or what to do. Naturally I wanted the animals. I could easily find a good home for Whiskey. In fact, he would have loved to be boarded and be around a bunch of equine friends. However, I did not have a property for the buffalo or the money to purchase one. I would have to lease a pasture that would have adequate fencing or provide fencing, or find a buffalo hobby ranch where I could take them. However, moving them anywhere, even to a buffalo ranch would be risky and complicated, requiring a well thought out plan and experienced handlers with equipment . . . and more money.

The thought of someone else buying The Kids was heart wrenching. The thought of never seeing them again was even worse. Most importantly, the stress of moving Billy while he was still weak was not safe for him. I explained to Gary, that the ideal situation would be to move the buffalo, when Billy was well enough, to a buffalo herd on vast acreage where he and his family could live out their lives as naturally as possible. But with

Billy being small for a buffalo male, I was concerned he could be in danger of being bullied and hurt by other males. I consulted with some buffalo ranchers, and they confirmed that could indeed be a problem.

At this point, I felt Gary was never going to adequately care for The Kids, and the focus was to get them somewhere else . . . anywhere else where they would be safe.

I told Gary that I would look for acreage or a ranch, but I would need time. I also asked him how much he would want for the animals, because I would have to figure out some way to get the money.

I also told him that he should consider whatever was best for the animals. If someone else could provide a better environment for them than I could, I would want them to go there and hope I could still see them. That sounded so noble, but the selfish part of me didn't really mean it. I couldn't imagine losing contact with The Kids. Separating me from Billy would be absolutely devastating to us both.

Gary never told me how much he wanted for his "pets," or when he would be ready to let them go. He said the other buyer was a neighbor down the street, who owned a huge, longhorn bull. Unbeknownst to Gary, I knew who he was talking about. I knew Gary hated his neighbor Bob because of a previous confrontation they had over the care of his buffalo, and he would never sell them to him. Gary was playing me.

He mentioned that he bought Whiskey from a friend for $300. I asked Jack Arnold how much Whiskey was worth and he said, "In this economy, you couldn't give him away." He said a Jack Donkey (that's no relation to Jack, it means an unaltered donkey) has to be separated from any mares, which creates an additional problem for that animal to be sold. When I told Jack that Gary said he paid a friend $300 for Whiskey, suggesting that would be his asking price, Jack laughed, "Well either Gary doesn't have any real friends or he is just plain dumb . . . but more than likely he is just trying to cheat you." Jack never skirted the truth as he saw it.

I didn't know which tactic Gary was using . . . The Carrot or The Stick? Was he waiving The Carrot in front of me, threatening that someone else wanted to buy the animals so I would be more eager to buy them? Or was he trying to ensure I would continue to take care of them, with The Carrot being owning The Kids at some future time when he was ready to let them go? Or was The Stick being used as a threat to sell them to someone else, in order to get the highest price from me? No doubt Gary was playing his hand, but which one? What exactly did he want?

A few days later Gary revealed his motives. He came up with the splendid idea that we should buy his place; then we wouldn't have to worry about finding a property for the animals, he wouldn't have to sell them to someone else, nor would I have to worry about moving Billy.

Gary thought he had come up with the perfect solution. Not only would he be able to sell the animals at his own set price, but he could also unload his property. He never really believed that we were a lot worse off financially than he was. He also didn't realize that there was nothing even remotely enticing about his unhealthy, dilapidated property that we referred to as, The Concentration Camp.

It was then I knew that Gary was not only carrying The Big Stick, but he was waving it ominously over my head, and I had better tread carefully. Gary knew he had me over a rodeo barrel, but it was one of my own choosing. I loved every dusty, hot minute of caring for The Kids and never resented it. What I was beginning to resent was being played for a sucker, and having to constantly dodge The Big Stick he was waving while having to pretend not to see it. However I was prepared to accept anything and everything in this precarious situation until Billy was healthy. I would not do anything to jeopardize his recovery.

Fall was approaching, when our businesses historically are busier. Robert and I had arranged our schedules that summer so at least one of us would be in Grass Valley to feed The Kids. There were days when I drove 5 hours round trip from the Bay area just to feed them. I recall only missing four days out of the summer, and then I practically begged Gary to feed them, and made sure there was plenty of food in the barn. For two of those days, there was no evidence that he did. All that was required was a short walk to the barn to throw out some hay and to walk back home.

I had not known what carrot to offer Gary to get him to take care of his animals, but now it was clear that money would move him. Unfortunately, that was something I had too little to offer. At that point, I wanted to take that stick he was waiving over my head and smack him with it.

However, I would do nothing that might interfere with taking care of Billy.

My Love Affair with Buffalo Billy

Whiskey's Attempts at Desegregation

Whiskey, AKA "Mr. Social", had decided to make the best of a strange situation. It is extremely dangerous to have a donkey and buffalo living together. There are many sorry tales of horses being gored by buffalo. Buffalo, being fiercely socially connected to their herd families, just do not care for outsiders hanging around. They will accept but ignore an occasional deer or elk wandering by, but "hangers-on" just would not ordinarily be tolerated.

Whiskey was one of the most loving and social creatures I have ever known. He thrived on attention and interaction, and he did his best to gain acceptance into Billy's buffalo family. I never knew anything about donkeys when I met Whiskey, but I have since learned that they are gregarious by nature. However, at Billy's Place, Whiskey had no other donkey or horse buddies to hang with. Napini clearly did not like him and it was one of her favorite pastimes to harass him. Billy had no use for Whiskey either and basically tried to ignore him most of the time. It was obvious that they thought of Whiskey as an inferior creature to themselves. Apparently, they had never heard that in the Old Testament, God spoke to His people through a donkey. If God wanted to speak to us today, I know He would choose Whiskey as His spokesman.

Not only was the living situation dangerous for Whiskey, it had to have been lonely. Fortunately little Minko came along, and before she figured out that Whiskey wasn't a buffalo, he was a fun playmate, and she finally gave Whiskey something resembling a buddy. Napini would tolerate this oddball arrangement only because there just wasn't anyone else to entertain Minko. However, Napini never did show Whiskey any appreciation for his many hours of patience, babysitting for her.

When I first started feeding The Kids at the fence, Napini and Billy would get most of the food. Napini was always greedy for a good meal, and Minko had to be careful to work around her mom, to avoid The Horn or a head butt. Whiskey was used to being ostracized at mealtime, so he learned to leave the buffalo and stand on the other side of a bus stop hut that had been built at the end of the fence.

The daily feeding ritual began with my feeding Billy first, and then Napini would join in. While they were eating, I would run past the hut and feed Whiskey. If I took too long and made Whiskey wait, he would start hoofing at the dirt, making quite the dust bowl racket. I would race over to him with some food, heading right into this dust cloud, throw down the food, and then run back to give the buffalo their next course. It didn't take Minko long to figure out that she would get more food dining next to her childhood homey rather than next to her food aggressive mom. So, Whiskey and Minko would happily eat side by side. But after a couple of months, Minko's buffalo instincts kicked in, and she started to bully Whiskey about sharing their food. Poor Whiskey learned the lesson that childhood friends don't always translate well into adult friends, and he would have to kick up his back legs to get her to back off. This worked for a while, until Minko started to outweigh him. Most of the time they still got along, but occasionally even the best of friends can get on each other's nerves, especially during a challenge over who gets the most apples or sweet cob.

I could see that Whiskey was increasingly getting frustrated with Minko growing up and beginning to act more like a buffalo than a pal. He still wanted to be best friends, and he longed for things to be the same as they were before. But the handwriting was on the barn door wall. Pretty soon it was going to be three against one. Whiskey was just not a buffalo. So Whiskey decided to try the "If you can't beat 'em, join 'em" approach. He made every effort to desegregate Billy's Place, in the peaceful and persistently tactful manner of Martin Luther King. He would follow the buffalo up the hill in the afternoons, where they all took their naps together. He would wallow in their wallowing holes. If the buffalo happened to poop or pee in unison, he tried to join the action. But as hard as he tried, he just could not speak their language, or be as stoic and pondering as they were. He was too fun loving and outgoing for the buffalo way of life. I think he finally reached a point where he gave up trying to attain the ethnic equality he had tried so hard to achieve.

I could tell he was lonely, and I tried to give him more attention. He developed this habit of biting my clothes, which was really painful if some skin got in the way. It was his way of connecting with you and holding onto you as long as he could. I have never experienced a sadder loneliness than from this adorable donkey.

Whiskey and The Girls were getting healthy and looking more beautiful every day. My entire focus was on Billy's health now and trying to find a really good home for The Kids. I wanted to be ready to place them when Gary gave the word. I joked about having interviews for donkey pals for

Whiskey so he would have the most fun, and live out his life with really good equine friends. However, it was important to find a place far out in the country. To have a bunch of donkeys screeching happily together in a HEE-HAW singing party would surely violate any municipal noise ordinances, and I wouldn't want Whiskey landing in the pokey. If I had to come visit him there, the jailers would probably confiscate the carrot gifts as contraband. That would cause Whiskey to HEE-HAW even more, and I would never get him out of there.

I wanted so much to take Whiskey home. We lived on just shy of an acre, but the deed restrictions prohibited horses. Whiskey loved everyone and everything, and would easily adapt anywhere if given enough love and attention. However around our house, Ralphie liked being the only kid. And with his personality, even at only 60 lbs. and being 16 inches high, he would be asserting himself as The Boss, or he would try to teach Whiskey to throw the ball for him. Everyone had to throw the ball for Ralphie.

Whiskey living at our house would also mean all the flowers I planted would be eaten or trampled. But I would have gladly given up all the flowers in my yard for Whiskey's company. I thought about how I might be able to bend the rules to be able to keep him on our property. Could I pass him off as a Seeing Eye donkey? A mutantly large dog? A stray wild donkey just visiting? A deformed deer? But as much as I wanted to keep and love on Whiskey, it just wouldn't be fair to him. He needed equine buddies, as well as human ones. Someone had to provide the carrots, and someone had to know how to properly HEE-HAW at just the right tone as not to be "pitchy." Whiskey was so special, he deserved the best, and I wanted to find it for him.

My Love Affair with Buffalo Billy

It Was Time for The Talk

I decided that it was time to speak with Nevada County Animal Control. I did not want to get Gary in trouble. I just wanted him to feed his animals or to let them go. I could not be traveling to the Bay Area not knowing if the animals were being taken care of properly. Napini, Minko and Whiskey had gained weight and were looking really good, but Billy was still fragile and frail.

I reasoned that Animal Control could talk to Gary about the care and feeding of his animals, Billy in particular, prompted by a call from a concerned animal Good Samaritan. If Gary thought that Animal Control would be looking over his shoulder, and he would be held responsible for lack of care, perhaps he would finally step up to Billy's plate. I had no other options. Nothing else had worked and Gary would not fully commit to letting them go. I felt I was in limbo, but it felt more like purgatory, and we were at a dead end.

I had no experience dealing with Animal Control, but everyone I had spoken to who had dealt with them did not speak highly of them. That was the primary reason I decided instead to help Gary from the beginning. I believe individuals should take responsibility for things that need help if they have the capability. Government is frequently not the best answer and should sometimes be the last resort.

I contacted our county supervisor, Ed Scofield, to arrange an introduction to the manager of Animal Control, Sgt. Fevenger. If Animal Control was as bad and uncaring as people had said, I needed the added incentive of a supervisor involved who could do some follow up. I briefly told Ed the situation and he generously volunteered to give Fevenger a briefing and to expect my call.

I set an appointment with Fevenger and explained the situation. I asked that an officer talk to Gary about the animal's nutritional needs, and I offered Dr. Mario's contact information. I explained that we should give Gary the benefit of the doubt and hopefully, with law enforcement contacting him, it would make him realize his responsibility to the animals. I reiterated that I had tried every other avenue before coming to him but without success. I asked to rely on Fevenger's discretion, as I did not want Gary to know that I had spoken to him. I could not jeopardize having access to Billy while his health was so tenuous.

It was very clear that Fevenger wasn't interested in my dilemma or in Billy's. Government employees seem to think that we don't know when they are patronizing us. Some have done it for so long that they start believing they are good at it. It is a dance we sometimes play with them, trying to pretend they are not such terrible dancers while trying to avoid stepping on their toes.

Is it arrogance and lack of accountability coming from the top that festers in many government agencies? Since supposedly we are the government, isn't it up to us to hold them accountable? Sometimes the legal system is required to hold government accountable if our efforts fail to do so. In our case, because Animal Control was a department of law enforcement, it would be ironic to have the legal system force law enforcement to uphold the law and the very responsibilities for which we, as taxpayers, pay them.

After I left Fevenger's office, I felt a battle was brewing. Little did I know it would be more like a war.

Playing Chicken

Buffalo love to run. They don't have to have a reason for it, they just love doing it. Maybe they like to feel the ground beneath their feet rumbling and vibrating into submission, or they enjoy the fluid motion coming from their huge bodies that look so unlikely to possess such graceful movement. Or maybe it's just because it's fun.

It's an amazing thing to watch them run, and when they suddenly dart around an object at 35 miles an hour with such precision and agility, it's a thrill to behold.

I have read where bison have been observed actually playing games in the snow. A group of buffalo were seen at the top of a snowy hill. They took off running and then slid down. Then they'd run back up the hill and repeat the game. Don't tell me these animals don't think or feel emotion.

At first, we never saw the buffalo run because they were simply too weak and didn't have the energy. But one afternoon in late August, after they had finished their dinners, Minko turned away from us and just started running. Napini felt her joy and she turned and ran after her, past the barn, up the hill, turning around on a dime and then raced back down in full throttle. Little Minko was trying to keep up, with her little head bobbing up and down, side-to-side, in buffalo glee.

Napini was headed straight for a big oak tree running at full speed with a cloud of dust kicking up behind her. Robert and I both gasped when she was just seconds away from running head on into it. But just at the very last second, she darted to the side, and once past it, darted back on her original straight path without missing a stride. It happened so fast and so fluidly that we wondered if we had actually seen it. The Girls had a twinkle in their eyes as they played chicken with that tree. Robert and I had just as much fun watching them, like proud parents at their children's track meet.

We had never seen that kind of excitement in their eyes before that day, and we realized that they were well on the road to recovery.

However, the contrast in Napini and Minko's progress compared to Billy's was becoming more evident. Billy was not recovering. When he saw me drive up, he would take a quick, few, half energetic steps, but it was all he could muster. His willing and joyful heart wanted so much to overcome his uncooperative body. I had promised him I would make him well, but he was lagging behind. Billy's diarrhea was beginning to worsen, and it was time to call Dr. Mario back again to heal my boy.

I asked Gary if I could call Dr. Mario to look at Billy. Gary said, "Yes, I am worried about him too."

I called the vet and explained Billy's condition. I was devastated when Dr. Mario said, "I think we'd better check for Johnes' Disease." We set an appointment, and I informed Gary, explaining what Johnes' Disease was and what it would mean. When Dr. Mario arrived at Billy's Place for the appointment, Gary was nowhere to be found.

Dr. Mario retrieved a sample of Billy's diarrhea to test for a foreign parasite that might not have responded to the standard dewormer and to test for Johnes. He explained that since there wasn't a handling facility on the property, he could not obtain a blood sample from Billy to do extensive testing. He felt that anesthetizing him to draw some blood would be too dangerous in his condition. I felt Billy was slipping away, and I could do nothing to hang onto him. I wanted to do everything and anything to find a cure for this mystery illness that was stealing my boy. Dr. Mario prescribed major daily doses of Pepto Bismol for the diarrhea and said the Johnes test would come back in about ten days.

So twice a day I drove to Billy's Place with twenty two Pepto Bismol tablets stuffed into pieces of watermelon. I had not seen Billy drinking, and with his diarrhea, there was the threat of him dying from dehydration. So I would call to Billy, and like the sweetheart that he was, he came and ate the watermelon for me, so at least he would have the fluid from the melon. His tongue would be coated with the chalky pink pills, and it could not have tasted good. I knew he was eating it for me, and I loved him for it. I told him he had to eat the pills so he would get better. Billy tried so hard, and I tried even harder. My feeling of helplessness was overwhelming. After several days the Pepto Bismol was not helping, and I contacted Dr. Mario again.

Poor Dr. Mario had done everything he could do, although not ever really knowing what to do. It must have been so frustrating for him dealing with a suffering buffalo as well as a suffering Auntie, yet he was always so responsive, professional and caring.

Gary never did pay for any vet visits to help Billy get well, but he did thank me for paying for them. Thanks is a nice word but I needed more than that. My creditors wouldn't accept a thanks instead of payment, and Billy wouldn't get better from words and good intentions.

Buffalo Love

There is no mistaking a buffalo in love, and it's always the males that are consumed by it. The myth of Cupid's arrow entrancing it's victims with overwhelming passion is no myth when it comes to a buffalo struck in love. The males turn into 1500 to 2000 lbs. of quivering Jell-O once they have carefully chosen just the right one.

A male buffalo in love will not leave his intended's side. If she moves a few feet away from him, he will move the same. If she decides to lie down, well that was what he was thinking to do too. He will show his affection by gently nuzzling and nudging his beloved, and you can see how he adores her in his big expressive eyes. She sees it too.

While there is a courtship ritual with almost all animals, a male buffalo does not waste time and energy showing off to the female of his desire in order to get her attention and acceptance. Typical courtship with males in the animal world involves all sorts of contortions, squawking, and ridiculous behavior to attract a female and ward off other suitors. But buffalo are smarter than that. He focuses on showing his noble intentions with unwavering love, sweet affection, complete devotion and doting admiration. Unless another suitor charges or challenges him, he will not leave her side.

What female of any kind could resist that behavior? It's what every female wants: to feel loved, admired and protected. All men should take a lesson from what the buffalo already know. Divorce lawyers would be forced to give up their Porsches or find other occupations.

I've watched this courtship many times in Yellowstone and on private ranches. The males are all the same: pitifully needy, loving, and head over hooves with determination. However, the females know they are in charge. They react with either flattered annoyance or they thoroughly enjoy all the attention with just the right amount of coyness. It's all about old-fashioned courtship. But even the most hard to get bison debutante eventually comes to appreciate this all-consuming display of love and heeds the call of nature. After all, he is a buffalo and he will never give up. It is this spirit that allowed him to survive many a hardship for thousands of years. Being patient for a few days to win a sweetheart playing hard to get is no major obstacle.

Billy and Napini on the other hand, were a devoted couple. They were all they had until Minko came along. Billy did not have to court Napini.

She was crazy about him and most of the time they were inseparable. But just as in human relationships, sometimes too much togetherness requires some time apart. At times, one of them would walk to the other side of the pasture, but they would always be within sight of each other. Needing some space to buffalo doesn't mean being all alone.

Napini would have this wild eyed look most of the time that kept everyone uneasy, and seldom did she seem happy. But just when she made me angry by charging me at the fence, or she'd butt Minko away from eating, or she'd drive Billy crazy with her pushiness, there was something sad about her that made us all forgive her. She was just one unhappy girl. After all, she and her family had been almost starved to death, were confined to this dung filled, bare dirt plot of ground where a buffalo could not roam, her adored mate's health was slowly deteriorating, and it was up to her to take responsibility and take care of her family. Having to bear all that pressure was not in Napini's nature. That much stress would make any female cranky, and to make matters worse, this "other woman" arrives on the scene and was getting and giving way too much attention to her man. Any red-blooded female would feel jealous and lash out now and then. With Napini, however, it was increasingly becoming more now than then.

One evening in mid-August, I arrived at the usual spot along the fence where the buffalo three-some were waiting for me. I popped open my trunk and offered Billy a carrot. He refused. I thought to myself, "Is he not feeling well, or maybe he is just not in the carrot mood today?" While Napini and Minko eagerly ate their carrots, I offered Billy the three-grain hay, which had been his favorite the last few days. He backed away. I asked him "Sweetie, what's the matter?" He seemed distracted and not the slightest bit interested in having a conversation. As Napini and Minko began eating the three-grain hay, I received my answer. Billy put his chin on Napini's back. I thought "He's not . . . No he won't. . . . Not right in front of me! Oh my God he is!" I backed away from the fence knowing I could be in real danger. I did not want to be near a combined 2000 lbs. of uncontrollable buffalo passion. Napini backed away from the fence and a few feet away from Billy. He approached her again, put his chin on her back and attempted to perform his marital duty. The largest land mammal in North America can crush anything in its lovemaking path, so I stood as far back as I could without standing in the street.

Buffalo tend to be very private about their sex lives. In fact some ranchers have never actually seen it done. But not my Billy. He wanted his Auntie right there with him sharing in the event. We were family, after all. I just stood there dumbfounded. While Billy was doing his part to fulfill his husbandly responsibility, Napini wasn't quite sure about it, maybe not quite in the mood. She walked a few feet and stopped, trying to make up her mind. Billy was weak and frail, and without her full cooperation, it became increasingly difficult to continue to jump as high as he needed to in order to complete the love mission. This "on again, off again" affair continued all the way back to the barn. It was getting darker by the minute and I could not tell if Billy had succeeded. But suddenly, Napini turned around in a rage and began attacking him! She was completely out of control. As he ran to get away from her, she chased him with a vengeance. He ran past me with his tongue hanging out and a terrified look in his eye, with Napini racing behind him trying to ram him with her horns. They ran full speed around the perimeter of the pasture a second time, and I thought they were going to charge right through the fence, but at the last second Billy turned and ran past me, looking over with pitiful eyes. This physical exertion was too much for him in his condition and he was showing signs of tremendous stress. I felt helpless and could only yell at Napini to stop, and wave my arms to get her attention away from Billy. However, her rage would not be distracted. At first, little Minko thought this was some kind of fun tag game and tried to run with them. She soon realized the terror in it and ran up the hill to the big oak tree and stood next to Whiskey for safety.

Finally Billy had nowhere else to go for help but into the barn. Napini followed him in, and I heard bodies thrashing into the barn walls. Billy raced out and ran the perimeter of the fence again, with Napini angrily in pursuit. I was beside myself with concern for poor Billy and screamed myself hoarse. He ran back into the barn, but by that time it was dark, and the barn was pitch black. I could only hear two huge animals kicking and pounding into the walls. There was nothing I could do but pray Billy would survive this aggression.

Why had Napini turned on Billy? Did he accomplish his duty, and she was angry at something he did? Or was he not able to perform, and she was angry and frustrated? Did Napini know instinctively that Billy was ill, perhaps suffering, and she was going to hasten his end?

That night I barely slept. Every half hour I looked at the clock, whose hour hand seemed frozen. All I could think about was my precious boy and pray he was not harmed. I also tried not to be angry at Napini for what she had done. I kept thinking, "She's a wild animal. It's not her fault." But I just could not understand why she turned on Billy so viciously.

I rushed to my car as soon as it was light and drove in a fog of fear to what I might find. As I drove up, Billy was lying in the pasture under the metal cover. I was relieved that he was still alive. Napini was standing about ten ft. away from him. I approached saying, "Billy, Honey, are you alright?" He stood up slowly, weak from the ordeal with scratches on his hide but not bloodied. As he started to walk toward me, Napini bolted toward him aggressively. I yelled as loud and as mean as I could, "NO! Napini NO!" and I jerked my arms around forcefully. Napini stopped. As Billy started to walk toward me again, she ran up to him and jumped on his back. I again screamed, "NO! STOP THAT RIGHT NOW!" She stopped, walked over to Minko and started to jump on her back! Minko looked as surprised as I did and ran from her mom. I yelled again, "NO! NO! NO!"

For the next half hour I was yelling at Napini to prevent her from harming her family. Billy looked over at me at one point with eyes saying, "Thank you Auntie."

Finally Napini decided her obnoxious behavior, whatever she was trying to accomplish, wasn't working, and she walked off to the other side of the pasture and lay down in defeat. Sweet little Minko went over to console her mom and lay down next to her, nervously watching to see if there would be any more aggression. Buffalo compassion and forgiveness is boundless.

I got Billy to drink as much as he would, fed him to help get his strength back and then left him to rest.

I called Jack and described what happened with Napini attacking Billy and asked if he had ever experienced or heard of anything like that with cattle or any other animal. He was baffled, since he said it's the males that are usually aggressive. But from then on he jokingly referred to Napini as "that Jezebel."

No one knows what nature had told Napini to do or why, but it was a frightening and confusing experience of wildness that left Billy even weaker.

The Best Day and The Worst Day

A week later on Friday evening, I arrived to feed The Kids as usual, but Billy was not waiting for me at the fence. I spotted Napini pacing around the barn in a strange and tentative way. She seemed agitated and confused. Little Minko was trying to follow her mom's pacing steps and seemed even more disoriented. I looked for Billy but he was nowhere in sight. I held my breath, my eyes searching frantically for my boy. I began running to the barn calling out his name. I looked in his empty stall, around the side and back of the barn, and up the hill. My heart was pounding. I ran up to Gary's house and yelled out to him. He came out and I looked hard at him and said firmly and deliberately, "Where is Billy," as if some terrible secret were being kept from me.

Gary said, "He's in Whiskey's stall." I turned around and briskly walked to the barn, as Gary ran after me explaining that Napini had attacked Billy again. He said he tried everything to stop her, but she was relentless. Billy had run into Whiskey's stall, exhausted to get away from her. Gary and his brother were able to board up the entrance to separate them. I found Billy standing in the stall, looking frighteningly frail. He looked the worst I had ever seen him . . . like a walking skeleton.

I said to him, "Oh, Honey, are you okay?" He looked over at me with all the effort he could muster.

Gary had put a big plastic water bin in the stall, but Billy wasn't drinking. He wanted to get out of that claustrophobic stall that was only about 8 ft. x 10 ft., which was barely big enough for him to turn around. Napini came and stood by the boarded up entry and started pacing. Ordinarily, those nailed boards would not have been a match for a buffalo. Billy pushed his head into them, trying to get out, but he was too weak to budge them. I opened the 3 ft. half door to the stall and said, "Come here, Angel." He slowly came over and ate some sweet cob from my hand. Then he started to lean into me and the door. I felt so bad having to push him back, as I struggled to close it. He gave me a hurt look, but I could not take the chance of him getting out. I spoke gently to him and urged him to come take more food, which he did. But he clearly was very ill and only ate a few handfuls. I knew he would get weaker if he didn't eat or drink, so I kept encouraging him with loving words. He was watching Minko and Napini who were standing right outside the stall, wanting to join them, yet too tired to try. But he was more than tired. For the first time I knew Billy was dying.

Fear flooded over me. It seemed like I had dove into a huge pool of overwhelming fear. I felt immersed in it, and there was no sound. There only existed a frightening silence about everything around me, and I was paralyzed and drowning, sinking to rock bottom.

I spent a few moments in what felt like suspended animation. But how could I help Billy if I were drowning? I had to shake it off. I could not let my despair take hold of me. I promised Billy I would bring him back to health, and I just could NOT fail him. I would have to hold my breath in that drowning pool and keep fighting to swim to the surface.

I began walking back to my car to retrieve my phone to call Dr. Mario, when Gary stopped me to say he was headed out of town for the weekend. I spotted his wife standing sheepishly near the house. He told me his sister and his mother would remain home and he was glad that I would be there to look after Billy. I told him I was calling Dr. Mario and he nodded. But I was so angry and shocked that he would want to go out of town now. How could he even enjoy being away with Billy dying? But with my anger, there was also relief. With Gary gone, I would not have to tread lightly over what I said or did with Billy. I would not have to listen to any excuses or deal with his inaction. I would be making the life and death decisions about my precious boy, and that is how I wanted it. I carried the weight of a huge and frightening responsibility with possibly terrible consequences. But I was prepared to do whatever it took to save him. . .or God forbid. . . not let him suffer.

As I walked along the fence to my car, Napini ran up along side of me, which was something she had never done. Instead of giving her comfort, which I am sure she was seeking, I yelled at her, "Are you happy now? You may have killed him. Are you happy now?" My anger would not let me feel the hurt that was in her eyes from my venting. I was completely selfish in my own pain. She turned from me and walked slowly back to the barn to stand vigil outside Billy's stall.

How cruel we can be when our hearts are breaking. Nappy's heart was breaking too, and she only did what nature had told her to do. Nappy always was, and always would be, truly wild. How ridiculous and mean to blame her. Besides, after the blaming is done, there is still no relief from the pain that caused it.

After leaving a desperate message for Dr. Mario, I went back and stayed with Billy. I told him I was there and always would be. I told him how much I loved him and treasured him, and that I would try everything to help. As he watched me speak the words spilling out of my heart, I was sinking. So was he.

That night, Dr. Mario responded that he was out of town, but he arranged for another ruminate vet to see Billy the next day. I thought, "A ruminate vet? I needed a bison expert!" But there was not one in the entire state of California.

I left a message for Dr. Carlson on Saturday morning, pleading with him to come as soon as he could. I got in my car to go to Billy's Place and as I drove on that tense, winding road, I was afraid Billy had not survived the night. When I arrived, I looked over at the stall. . . he was standing! I thanked God, and ran to the barn. I greeted him cheerfully as if nothing were wrong. But Billy looked even worse. I tried coaxing him to eat, but he had little interest.

Throughout the day I exchanged calls with Dr. Carlson, making sure his schedule included Billy, even though he told me his schedule was full. I stayed with Billy, trying to comfort him, trying to get him to eat just a few more handfuls and giving him watermelon to keep him hydrated. Buffalo are highly affected by stress, which can shut down their immune systems. Confinement and separation is a main stressor for bison, so it was a catch 22. Billy needed to be with Nappy and Minko but I couldn't take the chance that she would turn on him again.

Nappy was starting to panic too. She was getting more agitated by the hour. She would pace outside the stall, stand and look forlornly at Billy and then start pacing again. She had a real fear in those beautiful brown eyes. I tried to get her to eat, but she would have none of it. She mock charged me with a stern warning. I knew how she felt. I couldn't eat anything either. I could barely take a full breath. The air we were all breathing was thick and polluted with fear and apprehension.

Gary's sister had her three year old grandson visiting. I left Billy to go feed Minko at the fence, as Napini stood stoically, looking agitated about 30 ft. away. The little boy suddenly ran up, touching the fence. In a split second, Napini bolted with her tail straight up, head down, running directly for the child. His eyes were as big as golf balls and I yelled, "Get back!" Gary's sister grabbed him and pulled him away, just seconds before Napini reached the fence and bent it out, nearly going through it. Had the boy not been pulled back when he was, he could have been killed. Napini could easily have gone through the fence had she wanted to. In her own way, she was yelling at the world and looking for someone to blame too.

Dr. Carlson arrived around 5 pm. I immediately felt he was genuinely concerned and was ready to help. He told me that Billy's tests had just come back and he did not have Johnes Disease. It meant there was hope. But hope was fading as fast as was Billy, and we were no closer to finding out what was wrong with him. I told Dr. Carlson we had to try everything, anything to help him. Dr. Carlson said the only thing he could think to do would be to administer a strong antibiotic. If only we could get a blood test to know what was wrong, but there were no handling facilities there to safely get a sample. Dr. Carlson suggested we sedate Billy, and he might be able to draw blood. We recognized this course of action was our last hope of saving him.

Dr. Carlson explained that in Billy's weak condition a sedative could kill him. But if we did nothing, he would die anyway. I asked Gary's sister to get her brother on the phone. After all, Billy was his animal, and he should be consulted and make the decision. I told Gary what Dr. Carlson had said, and he agreed that we should sedate Billy and give him the anti-biotic. That was the plan, but handling a bison, even a critically ill bison, was still a challenge.

The vet prodded Billy from behind to see how responsive he was. As frail and weak as he was, he kicked his back leg into the barn wall with such force that the whole building shook. We all looked in amazement. Based on the power that came from this sickly buffalo, if a 1500 lb. healthy one decided to kick something, there would be no life, and physically little left to resemble the victim. It was a reminder of the sheer dominance of this animal, and that treating Billy was a very dangerous situation.

Dr. Carlson made an extension for the syringe out of a four foot plastic irrigation pipe and gave Billy the sedative. After it took effect, he gave him the antibiotic. But even with the sedative, Billy was alert enough that it was still too dangerous to draw blood. I asked the vet if there were electrolytes I could give Billy. He showed me how to administer the liquid by shooting it down his throat with a buffalo sized syringe.

Billy was not coherent when I told him good night. He looked worse, if that were possible. He was barely recognizable as a bison.

That night I could not sleep. The fear of losing Billy, my answered prayer, was overwhelming, and I prayed. I prayed the prayer of the desper-ate. I prayed for God to heal my precious Billy. I tried to make a deal with

Him that if He healed Billy, I would live my life better. I would promise God anything. I begged the Lord on my knees to save him. In the wee hours of the night, I was exhausted and finally came to the right place with God. I could not make the decision about Billy's fate. If it meant living and suffering, I had to let him go. I surrendered the decision to the One who knows. I finally went to sleep.

I woke up late, had a quick breakfast, and I went to pick a couple dozen apples for Billy from a tree down the street. Even though the sun was shining, it didn't feel sunny. Everything felt labored, and nothing felt right.

I wanted to be prepared if Billy passed away. I did not want to have any regrets. I thought about what I would take with me: scissors, note paper and pen, a small plastic bag, a sheet, a beautiful hand painted silk ribbon, and one of my favorite pictures of Billy and me.

I checked my voicemail. Gary's sister had called asking me to come right away. Billy was down, lying on his side. A buffalo can't lie on its side for long because the weight of its head can suffocate it. I felt so bad that I had slept so late when Billy needed me. Robert and I rushed out the door.

It was another quiet, somber ride to Billy's Place, as I remembered how much I used to love that ride with such excitement and anticipation to see The Kids. I was afraid to see Billy down. I couldn't bear for him to suffer. I ran to the barn, looked over the stall wall and he was lying still on his side. His eyes were closed but he was breathing. I said softly, "Good morning, Angel." He looked up at me with those sweet brown eyes. Without hesitation, I grabbed the stall post and lifted myself up and over the 8 foot wall separating us. It is amazing what adrenaline and sheer will can accomplish. Gary's sister, mother and Robert looked at me, shocked that I had effortlessly scaled that wall. But their amazement turned to concern as I knelt down, right next to my boy. I was as close to Billy as I had always longed to be. . . nothing between us but the trust and love we felt for each other. I had no fear kneeling next to him, and he looked up at me and stuck his tongue out as he licked the air. I bent down and kissed him and stroked his face saying, "Are you thirsty, Honey? Auntie is here and she will take care of you. Let's get your head up." I slid a bale of straw next to his face, and then grabbed his enormous head with both my arms to put his head onto the hay. I could not budge the weight. His poor emaciated head still weighed about 150 lbs. I leaned over Billy and said to myself, "I am going to do this. Lord, give me strength to help our boy." I said to Billy, "Auntie is going to move your head up, Honey" and then I pulled his mighty head up just enough to get the bale under the tip of his, chin. Then I moved the bale, with his head, inch by inch until he was comfortable and safe. "There you are precious. Is that better?" I said. He looked up at me with such trust in his eyes. He had completely surrendered to my loving care.

I looked up at Gary's sister and asked her to call the fire department to come help Billy sit up, just as Roger Brooks had done for Charlie. Robert had mixed the electrolyte solution and filled the syringes, throwing them down to me. I said, "Open up love bug. I'm going to squirt this down your throat. You'll feel better." I slid the syringe in his mouth and squirted out the solution. Billy just kept looking into my eyes for comfort. Robert continued to fill the syringes as I emptied them in Billy's mouth. After I felt he had a substantial amount, I said, "Would you like to have some apple?" I put a big slice of apple, in his mouth and he ate it with pleasure. I kept talking to him softly and fed him about six apples. I asked Robert for more filled syringes. I said to Billy, "Okay, Honey, let's have more of this." He opened his mouth and swallowed the solution. Then, with a twinkle in his eye as he looked at me, he bit down gently on the syringe so I could not remove it. He was teasing me. As weak as he was, he wanted to let me know that our special bond was ever present. I chuckled and said, "You let go, you big goof!" He let go, and I continued giving him the electrolytes and the apples. I was feeling encouraged. But most of all, I was feeling grateful. Here I was with Billy in a stall not much bigger than the both of us. There was no barrier between us. None physical, none wild or human. I have never been happier in my life than in those precious few hours I spent next to Billy. Looking into his eyes, I saw his beautiful, wild yet innocent soul reach out to me. I gave him everything I had.

Gary's sister said the fire department was on the way. I told Billy to hold on, and that help was coming to lift him up. A couple of times he closed his eyes as I was stroking his face, and I looked over at his chest to make sure it was moving. I pleaded with him in a broken voice, "Hold on Billy. Stay with me, Honey. The entire fire department is coming to help, that's how important you are."

The fire department had also called Animal Control. A tough acting woman named Officer Falls walked into the barn and blurted, "'We've had a complaint about these animals. Evidently someone is feeding them because the owner isn't.'"

I thought, now is not the time to get into this. I said, "That person feeding the animals would be me." Gary's sister was indignant that anyone would question her brother. Robert directed Falls outside to speak with her alone. Five firemen arrived, but just when I was ready for heroes, they all lined up looking down at me, startled I was sitting next to a buffalo. They made it clear they were not getting in that stall with a buffalo. My husband explained the goal of getting Billy to sit up. He had tried to get up on his own, but all that happened were legs flailing and thrashing. I told Billy I would be back after he sat up, and I lifted myself out of the stall. The firemen didn't know what to do or how to do it. They were willing to help, but they were not willing to get near the buffalo. Robert grabbed a long board and suggested they wedge it under Billy. After it was in place, all six men pushed down on the board and it lifted Billy just enough to sit up. I thought we had accomplished something good, until I saw Billy's face. He looked so calm and peaceful lying down, but now sitting up, he looked pitiful. It nearly killed us all to look at him.

Dr. Carlson arrived with an assistant and began tending to Billy. Falls asked to speak to me, so I reluctantly walked outside with her and explained the sensitivity of the issue. I did not want to get Gary into trouble. I just wanted her to speak with him, when he returned, about properly feeding his animals. Nothing I had said or done had made a difference. At one point, she told me there was nothing she could do unless I stopped feeding the animals and they got dangerously thin again. I couldn't believe that anyone who works with animals would tell you to mistreat them so they could help them. I told her I could not do that. She shrugged her shoulders, and therefore gave the shrug to the problem.

In the meantime, Dr. Carlson got Billy to his feet. My momentary elation, turned to despair when I saw him fall back down, too weak to stand. I walked away, not wanting Billy to see me cry. Robert slowly approached me, and gave me the news I had been trying to defeat for over four months. He said with his head down, "Dr. Carlson says it's time to let Billy go. "My husband's face was so tortured as his mouth spilled out those horrible words. I felt so sorry for him to have to be the one to tell me. I looked down and nodded, thereby giving Billy his death sentence.

Dr. Carlson's assistant told me sometimes it is better not to watch, as wild animal's reactions can be violent. I couldn't speak. I just thought to myself, "She doesn't know my Billy. She did not know how he gently took a strawberry from my hand. She didn't know how he loved me to sit and talk to him and how I gave him lipstick kisses. But she did know for certain how much I loved him.

Trying to compose myself, I walked around the barn to say good bye to Billy. They had positioned him facing the pasture. I sat down by his sad, tired face and for the first time, stroked his wooly bangs. He just let me. I kissed his cheeks and nose and told him how sorry I was that I did not keep my promise. I told him how much I loved him, and thanked him for everything he had given me and taught me. . . especially about myself. I whispered that I would take care of Nappy and Minko, and that I would see him again. He was quiet and still. I stood up and looked at Robert, who had been standing behind me. He was crying too, and in that glance he knew I wanted him to stay with Billy, and I knew he wanted to.

I walked out into the open air, the blazing sun, and it surprised me that the world was continuing on just the same as it always does. I waited at the truck for it to be over. I was glad that Nappy and Minko had gone up the hill to rest so they wouldn't have to see Billy die. I took out the notepaper and pen and wrote a love note to Billy. I folded it up into a one inch square. I gathered up the sheet, the delicate hand painted silk ribbon, the scissors and plastic bag, and the picture of Billy and me. Robert walked out of the barn and nodded. Billy had died peacefully, just as he had lived.

I walked past everyone to be alone with my boy. They had tied a rope around his face. I said, "Oh Billy, we can't have an ugly old rope on my darling boy." I removed the rope and felt his warm body. It comforted me to feel his warmth. I knelt down beside him and tried to move his head to put the delicate silk ribbon around his neck. But just as before, his head was too heavy and I did not have any more strength from which to draw. I struggled to slip it under his neck and catch it on the other side. I slowly and gently tied it into a bow. I touched his horn, for the first time, like a priceless artifact. I examined every inch of it so I would not forget. I punched a hole in our picture and put it on his horn. I placed my love note deep in his ear, so it could not be lost or found. I cut off a piece of his wirey bangs. I felt how dense and thick they were, this amazing armor designed to cushion the heads of generations of dueling buffalo. I then looked toward Billy's adorable eyelashes, that always made me smile. I cut them off, and along with his bangs, put all that would be left of Buffalo Billy in the plastic bag and sealed it shut, I kissed him again, felt his hair against my cheek, and covered him with the sheet.

I left part of my heart there in that tiny stall. Gary's family was crying and hugging each other for comfort. Gary's mother put her arms around me and I sobbed, and then sobbed some more. But I really just wanted to go home to grieve alone. Falls came up to me and said she was sorry. I reminded her that she had agreed to request a necropsy, an animal autopsy, and I asked her to please follow up on it. If the necropsy pointed to neglect, would she pursue it? She said that she would. She seemed genuinely moved.

Dr. Carlson very sensitively approached me about payment for his services since I had paid for his visit the day before. I looked at him intently and said, "Dr. Carlson I would have paid any amount for Billy to live. I am not paying for him to die. Gary will pay that bill." The vet nodded and walked off toward Gary's sister. Robert and I drove home on that lonely road. He drove slowly and deliberately, as we could barely see the road through our tears. We greeted Ralphie at the door with special long hugs. I sat down to write Billy's Story. It was just a few paragraphs to describe all that he was, and all he had meant to me. It took me just a half hour to pour out my grief and gratitude. I e-mailed it to everyone who had heard about my love affair with the shaggy, beautiful beast I called Buffalo Billy.

Later that afternoon, I knew I had to go back to feed Napini and Minko. They would have known by then that Billy was dead and they would be in mourning. Their world as they knew it had ended and they needed as much normalcy as possible. Billy had left them and I did not want them to think I had too. I gathered the courage to drive back, but as soon as I saw the sheet in the stall, I cried. I cried as I fed Minko and Whiskey. I cried as I unsuccessfully tried to get distraught Napini to eat. I cried because Billy was never going to be there again. I cried all the more because I had failed to keep a promise that was not mine to give.

*Auntie strolling down the middle of the street wih her
DBFF (Donkey Best Friend Forever).*

The Great Escape and the Long Road Home

Billy had been gone for about two weeks, when I received a voicemail from Gary early on Saturday morning. The news could not have been worse. The buffalo and Whiskey had escaped from his property and were missing.

I immediately called him back to say we were on our way. We sped down the road thinking, "What could go wrong next?"

Gary showed us the back fence where Napini had hooked her horns and ripped the wire from the post. We had never seen the back fencing, but seeing it now, it would have been an easy obstacle to breach for a buffalo who wanted out. Jack Arnold had laughed about the inadequate fencing and showed me the wire was even put on the wrong side of the posts, leaving it further compromised. Gary had told me that Billy had escaped once before, and that his neighbor was upset because Billy had wandered into their pasture with their horses. Since it was the neighboring property, it wasn't so difficult to get Billy back. But this time was different. The escapees were now roaming the entire neighborhood of 5 to 10 acre parcels of steep terrain, with rocky hills 100 ft. in height, covered with heavy brush and trees. Finding the buffalo and containing them would be nearly impossible.

Since buffalo are very sensitive and family bonded, when a member of a herd family is lost, they will go into deep mourning, and sometimes stop eating. Because of this, buffalo rancher and former Yellowstone Game Warden, Bob Jackson, recommends that buffalo meat ranchers take whole families to slaughter as being the humane thing to do.

Napini had always been edgy and at times, aggressive, but since losing Billy, her emotions ranged from despair to outright aggression. There was no doubt that Nappy escaped, looking for her mate. Her life was turned upside down without him. Baby Minko and their pal, Whiskey, went along for the adventure.

With Napini roaming unfamiliar territory, with everyone being a stranger and dogs running freely on large tracts of land, it could be disastrous for anyone or anything who might spook or challenge her. If The Girls made their way onto those dark roads at night, an oncoming car would not see their dark brown figures until it was too late. . . too late for the animals and the passengers. If Animal Control became involved, they would not hesitate to shoot them if there were even the slightest confrontation. Furthermore, this was still the Wild West to some people, who would think shooting a buffalo would be sport.

Nappy was what a psychologist would call, passive aggressive. Basically she was a frightened animal who learned to cope by first being the aggressive one. She learned that if she were aggressive, most creatures would back off. But when challenged, unless it involved survival and to a lesser degree maternal instincts, Nappy would normally back down and run. She displayed this behavior on every occasion we stood our ground with her. But with her emotions running as wild as her natural character, the element of her unpredictability was even more worrisome. In any case, we had to find them before something bad happened. But if we found them, how would we contain them? I tried not to focus on the impossible dilemma before us. We just had to find them.

They had been spotted that morning in someone's yard. Imagine the shock of looking out your window and seeing two buffalo and a donkey mowing your lawn. Telling that story would be comparable to the beginning of a very funny joke. That was exactly what a neighbor reported to 911. I am sure the dispatcher asked the caller to repeat what she was hearing, "You have two buffalo and a donkey in your yard?". . . and happy hour wasn't even close to getting started.

The sheriff's department had been alerted and called Gary to report the address of their sighting, and we sped to the scene. We found the trouble-making trio inside an iron fenced yard. They were watching us get out of our trucks and wondering what to do next. I think they were as perplexed as we were. We all were making it up as we went along. Gary said, "What do we do now?" The homeowners were even more flustered as to what to do. I asked them to bring us a phone book to locate a livestock hauler, and I handed it to Gary. He nervously thumbed through the book standing at his truck, as Robert and I approached the animals slowly, talking to them calmly. Whiskey moved over to the husband/homeowner, never wanting to miss an opportunity to make a new friend.

I turned toward Napini and said, "Nappy, what are you doing here? Let's go home."

With that, she calmly walked toward us. Robert and I were both happy she responded, but we were scared to death. And what would we do when she came up to us? You can't put a rope around a buffalo's neck and lead it home. She continued walking closer, and we both moved next to big tree trunks, just in case things became dicey. But as we moved away from her, it upset her, and she bolted away to the fence. She became frightened and agitated and began running wildly back and forth along the perimeter of the fence, with Minko running just as confused behind her, trying to keep up. Napini began frantically thrashing into the iron fence to find a way out. We yelled to Gary in the driveway, "Close the gate!" But it was too late. Napini ran wild-eyed out the gate, with Minko following, and they quickly disappeared into the rugged brush. Our consolation was that Whiskey had stayed behind and seemed content to be done with the whole escapade.

Gary said, "Now what are we going to do?"

I said, "Let's get a trailer for Whiskey and take him home."

Gary responded that Whiskey had never been in a trailer, except when he first arrived and added, "That donkey is so stubborn, I doubt he'll go in. Let's just let him go."

I looked at him incredulously as Robert was shaking his head and said, "Gary, we can't just let him go. He may get hit by a car, and we may not have another opportunity to corral him if he rejoins The Girls.

Gary was not in favor of working with Whiskey to get him home. I said, "Look, let's at least try to get him in a trailer, and if we can't, we'll walk him home."

Gary was unmoved and said, "He'll never get into a trailer, and he's too stubborn to walk him. Besides, it's over 3 miles."

I looked at him intently, "Trust me. I'll walk him home. Do you know someone with a horse trailer?"

Gary reluctantly left to get a trailer and we stayed behind. We asked the property owner, who by now had become intimate friends with Whiskey, if he had some carrots or greens we could use as a trailer bribe. They good naturedly raided the produce section of their refrigerator, and we were armed with a donkey sized salad bowl filled with assorted leafy temptations.

After a half hour, Gary returned with a small open cart in tow. He said he could not locate a horse trailer. Robert and I looked at each other, Whiskey looked at the cart, and the three of us thought, "No way. This isn't going to happen." Gary said his "horse friend" told him if the donkey hadn't been in a trailer for six months, he would not go in. Not wanting to argue with stupidity, we decided to attempt futility. Even with the offer of tossed salad, which Whiskey accepted without apology, he was still NOT going in that open cart. I finally said to him, "I wouldn't either. How about taking a walk?"

Gary repeated, "Let's just let him go."

Robert answered, "Gary, let's just try it. I'll lead in the truck, she will walk with him and you follow in your truck. Or I'll walk him."

I said, "No, I'll do it." I looked at my new walking buddy and asked, "It will be fun. . . right, Whiskey?"

We were headed down a narrow, two lane country road where traffic would be a problem. We needed the two truck caravan with flashing lights to protect the two walkers. We put a rope around Whiskey and kept it loose, since he wasn't harness trained. I put my arm around his neck and said, "Okay Whiskers, let's boogey!" And with that, we began our after-noon hike. Whiskey was completely cooperative, and if he got a bit dis-tracted, I would wave a carrot in front of him, and he would continue his pace. However, he soon spotted two horses and stopped, looking at them longingly. I enticed him with a handful of tossed salad, and that inspired him to start up again. After walking about a mile, a truck pulled up, the window rolled down, and a man was laughing, "Out for a walk, are we?" We all laughed, waived, and they sped around us, having a great story to tell.

Whiskey was enjoying the freedom and the attention, and acted as if walking down the middle of the road was a perfectly normal thing to do on a Saturday afternoon. I was pointing out a couple of deer who were watch-ing us, when Whiskey spotted a better prize: a blonde bombshell of a mare standing in the pasture up the road. It was love at first sight, and he began trotting toward her.

I had made the mistake of wrapping his rope around my hand, so I involuntarily started trotting too. I was frantically trying to break free as Whiskey began to pick up speed. As the rope wound tighter and tighter around my hand, I became completely under his control with that rope binding us together. My husband saw what was happening, and he jumped out of the truck to grab the rope. But 500 lbs. of donkey love on the run is no match for two people. A picture passed through my mind of the typical scene in B western movies of the bad guy being dragged by a horse through a cactus filled range, tied to the end of a rope. I was picturing myself in that same role being drug by a donkey, except I had no stunt person. Luckily when my husband jerked the rope, that moment of slack allowed me to get my rope burned hand free.

Whiskey ran up to the mare, and they nuzzled each other's faces. No amount of carrots, salad, threats, or sweet talk would move Whiskey from his beloved. Gary ran up and pulled the rope around his neck with all his might, to no avail. We had to let Whiskey continue his courtship and figure out a way to get him moving again.

The two lovebirds flirted for another half hour, when suddenly the fickle filly darted off. Poor Whiskey stood heartbroken, but he wasn't about to give up hope and stood staring at her. I said, "Okay Romeo, can we go now?" Whiskey knew he would never see the lovely Juliet again and didn't want to say goodbye. Gary drove his truck up behind Whiskey, and between F-150 horse-powered metal and the pain of rejection, Whiskey was on the move again with his entourage. I put my arm around his neck to console him and began explaining that maybe he should act a little harder to get next time. I told him it wasn't his looks that was the problem or his outgoing personality…. he just needed more experience with the fillies.

Robert asked me if he could take a turn at walking Whiskey, so I jumped in the truck and lead the way. In my rear view mirror, I watched the two pals walking side by side, acknowledging all of the traveling admirers who passed by laughing, pointing, and waving. Normally, pointing and laughing would be considered bad manners, but Whiskey overlooked convention and soaked up the attention.

Whiskey had proven to be a good natured and willing walking buddy on what was his three miles of freedom. As we approached the house, our hearts sank that we were taking him back, and he would be all alone without The Girls for company. When we approached the pasture, I whispered to him that I was sorry, and I hoped we could get him to a home soon with other donkeys or horses. I knew my husband was thinking the same thing by the look on his face and his tender petting of Whiskey's nose.

It was special time with Whiskey I will never forget. But it was also sad to see how lonely he was for his own kind. He had to settle for buffalo pals who could not fulfill his needs and who never really appreciated him.

Gary thanked us for returning Whiskey, but he looked very distraught and lost. Our thoughts then turned to the buffalo. I put my arm around Gary and I said, "Somehow, this will work out. We will find them." Driving away, seeing Whiskey alone in the pasture with his head down, left us feeling empty. I didn't dare think about how we were going to capture The Girls. I would think about that tomorrow.

Where The Buffalo Roam

Momma and her calf on the lam

BY LIZ KELLAR
Staff Writer

Nevada County isn't normally known as a home where the buffalo roam.

But two were still on the lam Monday after first being sighted Saturday morning by bemused residents of Alta Sierra Ranches.

A buffalo cow and her calf, accompanied by a guard donkey, escaped from their enclosure on Dog Bar Road Saturday and were spotted on Tiger Tail and Buck Ridge roads. The donkey was recaptured.

Owner Gary said he had owned buffaloes for six years and never had any trouble with them.

But two weeks ago, his bull died from parasites, he said.

"The cow started going crazy. She got goofy," Gary said. "She started tearing things up, busting stuff. She eventually tore through the back fence — I assume, looking for the bull."

The cow took off with her year-old calf, and the pair was noticed to be missing Saturday.

"About 9 in the morning, I got a call from my neighbor asking me if I'd looked out the window recently," said Stuart Gold, who lives in the 19000 block of Buck Ridge Road.

When Gold's neighbor told

See BUFFALO A10

HAVE YOU SEEN THEM?

If so, call Nevada County Animal Control at (530) 265-7880. Use caution — buffalo are wild animals and can be aggressive.

BUFFALO:
Continued from A1

him about his large visitors, "I asked him if he'd been drinking," he laughed.

"I tried to approach them, but they were skittish, to say the least," Gold said. "They were happy to be out. Anytime I approached, they would run off."

According to Gary, the two buffalo were last spotted Monday morning at a pond on Wolf Creek Road. He went to look for them, but they already had moved on into thick woodland.

"We've had her cornered, but she's going to have to be sedated or shot," he said. "You can't get near her. She's gone wild, and the baby's just following her."

It's almost impossible to lasso an animal of that size, Gary said, adding he has hired a cattle rancher to help

Submitted photo by Stuart Gold

A buffalo cow and calf made a surprise visit to this Buck Ridge Road property Saturday morning and remained on the lam Monday.

capture her.

"Everybody's looking for them,"

To contact Staff Writer Liz Kellar, e-mail lkellar@theunion.com or call 477-4229.

The Beginning of the End

I had suggested to Gary that he contact the media about the buffalo on the loose. The residents in the area needed to know the danger, and hopefully spot them and report it so we could catch them.

Catch them? How do you "catch" buffalo? Maybe Billy and Minko could have been lured into cooperation, but Napini? Her current mood, ranging from sadness and despair to anger and confusion, were the normal emotions all grieving widows feel. Her naturally skittish nature would now be even more unpredictable with the uncertainty of unfamiliar territory. She was looking for Billy, and that was not going to be.

Everyone asked why Animal Control was not helping, since this was not only an animal problem but also a public safety issue. Robert was in phone contact with Sgt. Fevenger making sure he knew what actions we were taking. Robert was trying to coordinate our efforts by asking Fevenger for a commitment as to what they would actually do. Fevenger said he would send Officer Falls out to talk to Gary about relinquishing the animals, since he wasn't caring for them properly and obviously didn't have adequate fencing. Then Fevenger said they might tranquilize the animals. He told Robert a lot of things but none that actually happened. Fevenger had essentially taken off his pants and given them to Falls, whose agenda and whose pant size did not fit his.

Falls was quoted a few times in the local newspaper. She said she went to the area to look for the buffalo on one occasion, but that Animal Control would only get involved if there were a confrontation with them. Then she said they would come out and shoot them.

Falls was also quoted repeating her favorite publicly spoken four letter F word, "fine." She stated the buffalo were "fine" on the loose. She said, "They had plenty to eat and were enjoying themselves." Falls didn't know a thing about buffalo. All that woman had to do was look at the bone thin deer in the area to know there was not enough food to sustain the deer population, what's more a combined total of 1500 lbs. of buffalo. They were in an area of coyotes and mountain lions, as well as dogs and cars. These girls had never been on their own, and while their wild instincts would eventually kick in, it would be a very difficult and traumatic time. Not to mention, they were still in mourning, searching for Billy. I knew the stress and confusion Napini was feeling, and little Minko must have been frightened, staying tight with her mom for guidance and reassurance. Things were definitely not "fine."

It was up to me to solve this impossible situation that Gary created, that Animal Control wanted to ignore, and could mean the end for The Girls. Wild animals come to so many tragic ends because people do not know how to care for them, don't bother to find out, and don't know their requirements for containment. So many times, wild animals escape from an inadequate enclosure, and they end up paying a deadly price for it. I was determined that was not going to happen to Napini and Minko.

In order to attract The Girls, Robert and I put their feed around the pond where they had been spotted, and a wildlife expert from the San Diego Zoo recommended that I play recordings of buffalo grunts.

But if The Girls came to the pond, how would we get them into an enclosure to get them into a trailer? They were in hilly and heavy brush country on remote acreage. Fortunately, because there was a stream running through the area they would have water, which also meant the two fugitives could hide out indefinitely. The old saying "It's like finding a needle in a haystack" seems an unlikely analogy for finding two enormous animals in the brush, but it clearly defined the situation. It meant we needed a posse. We needed the media to report the escape so we could get a lot of volunteer eyes to help hunt for The Girls. I contacted Liz Keller from the local newspaper, The Union, and told her the story.

That night I thought about a plan to capture Napini and Minko. A plan to capture buffalo needs to include a plan B and a Plan C. Realistically with the dilemma we faced, I needed back up plans involving the entire alphabet. The more I planned different scenarios, the more hopeless it looked. We had saved The Girls and brought them back to health, but now I could lose them to a bullet from Animal Control or a car hitting them at night.

If we could get them into someone's corral with the lure of food, we'd have to be at just the right place at just the right time to close them in, which meant we'd need to camp out there. But what if they weren't in that area, but were somewhere else? We had no choice in locations because we'd be limited to corrals that were strong enough to contain a panicked and charging Napini. This wasn't a community of ranches using heavy equipment and with buffalo safe fences. We would also have to find a property owner willing to take on the responsibility involved.

We discussed the idea of tranquilizing Napini. If she were dragged into a trailer, Minko would go too. But with acres of high rugged hills, thick trees and brush with one road going in and out, she would have to be in just the right place to be tranquilized and then dragged into a trailer safely. Dragging a 1000 lb. dead weight could also mean serious injury in this rocky terrain. I located a tranquilizer gun from the UC Davis zoo department that had the only gun big enough for bison. But they would only release it to a veterinarian which created another problem. If Napini were spotted, I'd have to call a vet, who would then have to drop everything and drive to this remote spot and hope she would still be there when he arrived. Napini did not like strangers, and she would not stay around to meet one, what's more one carrying a high powered weapon.

The experts who gave their opinions, and even Jack Arnold, advised me that the buffalo would never return to the Concentration Camp once they were free. So we had to decide on a plan, get volunteers to help, and pray for our next buffalo miracle. It would take nothing short of a miracle.

Once we got the buffalo into the trailer, where would we take them? Gary said in a subsequent newspaper article that if they did return to his property they could escape his fence again and he wanted to be done with them. I obviously did not want them at his place either. I needed a destination where they could live out their lives, preferably roaming on vast acreage with other buffalo.

I did not focus on the impossibility of the situation, but instead the focus was on implementing the various scenarios that might work . . . and I prayed. I was becoming a real prayer warrior.

The next day we went looking for The Girls. We drove up and down the long, winding roads calling their names, talking to every neighbor we encountered. We put notices on people's mailboxes with our phone number and Gary's number. We did not find any sign of them and drove home at dusk, worried about them wandering onto the dark, unlit roads.

The next day the article came out in the paper. The Girl's story was a sensation, and people started calling me to help find them, to lend us their trailers, and one kind stranger, Althea Stuart, sent a check to help with the vet and transportation costs. It was so inspiring the way people cared about these girls. Everyone wanted them to be found and rescued. A Sacramento TV station caught wind of it and came out to interview Gary. In the following days, the local newspaper kept the story front page and kept a count down of the days that passed that the buffalo girls were still on the lam.

Another article came out a couple of days later, and I eagerly read it, wanting to make sure the phone numbers were listed if someone spotted them. As I was reading, my hands went numb and the paper fell to the floor. I could not believe what I had just read. Gary said he was contemplating having them hunted down and shot. He did not want the liability of buffalo running loose.

That was the beginning of the end for Gary. In spite of everything, I had given him every benefit of the doubt. I had given him every opportunity to do the right thing for his animals. I had made excuses for him, willingly helped him whenever he called. He had made me believe these buffalo were his pets. How could he shoot his "pets?" For Gary it was easier to just kill them rather than explore other options with me. That was just too much work compared to a quick couple of bullets to The Girls' heads. We had been looking for them for days, and since we never saw Gary, it was obvious now that he had been busy planning the easy and fatal way out of this dilemma of his own making.

My phone was ringing off the hook from people who wanted to volunteer to help find the buffalo and did not want this kind of ending. Gary had finally revealed who he really was to the entire County.

I contacted Gary's neighbor, Bob, who owned a huge long horned bull that his wife had tamed into the equivalent of an overgrown pony. Bob was the only one in the immediate area who had electrified fencing with a lot of acreage. Bob had stopped a few times while I was feeding the animals and had been appalled to see Billy in his condition. He had marched up to Gary's door and offered to buy the three buffalo right there on the spot. Bob had a good heart and a real soft spot for two things: his wife and animals. He was a cantankerous sort and really enjoyed confrontation. So when Gary refused to sell the buffalo to him, Bob did not hold back telling him what he thought of him. That resulted in a near fist fight, and from then on, the two of them hated each other. But I didn't care that there was bad blood between them. My only concern was getting The Girls somewhere safe, and I knew Bob had the fencing and the heart. Better yet, he would take The Girls just to irritate Gary.

I was out walking the streets looking for Napini and Minko, when Bob pulled up alongside me in his truck. He had been out looking for The Girls too. He did not know that Billy had died, and he was very upset. He asked me what had happened, and when I told him that Gary had left town the weekend Billy died, he went ballistic. He called Gary all the names I had wanted to call him, and even some I had never heard. Just about that time,

Gary's car came driving down the road. I was so hoping he wasn't in it, while Bob was so hoping he was.

Gary pulled up beside us with an angry contorted face and said to me, "What is HE doing here?"

Bob was thrilled at the prospect of taunting Gary and said, "I am looking for your buffalo you {*CENSORED*}" And then the war began. They began yelling at each other, as I tried to dodge all that testosterone flying back and forth. I was standing in the middle of the road between these two crazed men in their vehicles. Bob was controlled and enjoying the scream fest, while Gary was completely out of control angry.

Then Gary turned his attention to me and yelled, "So you are conspiring with the neighborhood crazy?!"

I thought to myself that I didn't know who was crazier, and I said calmly but forcefully, "I will conspire with the devil himself if it means saving those girls. Bob has been out looking for your animals just like we have, and you should be grateful!"

Then Bob couldn't help himself egg Gary on even more and said, "Well at least I don't kill MY animals!"

I thought Gary's eyeballs were going to explode. He pulled his car over and got out, walking menacingly toward us. My legs began to shake, but Bob remained calm and was grinning. Gary seemed ready to throw a punch, and I didn't want to be in the middle.

Bob just wouldn't quit and said, "I am no {*CENSORED*} who would leave my dying animal and go on a vacation!"

OUCH.

Bob's anger had just exposed me, and I knew that would be the end of any further communication with Gary. I had always stopped short of doing anything that would jeopardize caring for the animals, but Bob had forced me over the line I could not cross.

Gary looked at me and said, "So you are in this with HIM? I held out my arm hoping to stop him from lunging at me, trying to diffuse the situation if I could.

I said, "Well, I didn't exactly say that. I said you left for the weekend."

Bob's pleasure then suddenly converted into Gary's out of control anger and he said to me, "What? Are you backing down? You get me involved, and then you are backing down?"

Now I had two Spartans at war on either side of me, and I felt that I might end up being collateral damage. Bob drove off cursing us both, leaving me alone with Gary, who was not in a huff… he was raging. I felt very threatened, and I began walking swiftly to my car.

Thankfully Gary did not follow and marched back to his car and yelled, "You picked the wrong side!" and sped off. If choosing to protect his animals, along with the help of a man who genuinely cared about them meant I picked the wrong side, then I certainly did.

I hate to admit that I was shaking so hard my foot could not stay on the gas pedal, so I sat there to calm down. I was just thankful I was in one piece. For the next four months, screaming, profanity, and threats were going to be regular visitors in my life. For a person who hates confrontation, that would be a living nightmare.

The following afternoon, after we had spent the day looking for Nappy and Minko to no avail, Robert and I drove by Billy's Place to give some carrots and affection to Whiskey. We hoped Gary would not be home. No such luck. Gary and his sister came down the driveway to his gate. They were yelling at us to leave, and that we were no longer welcome. I had experienced my quota for the year of confrontation the day before, but Robert was not about to let Gary intimidate him. While brother and sister were screaming and yelling, calling the sheriff to report the heinous crime of someone feeding their donkey, Robert calmly finished feeding Whiskey the carrots he had brought, patted him on the face, and kissed him goodbye. Whiskey did not know that would be the last time we could visit for a very long time.

A week had gone by with no buffalo sightings. I was working to obtain the tranq gun from UC Davis and to hire Dr. Mario as the shooter. I was holding my breath that Gary was not going to kill those girls. But knowing him as I did, I knew he wouldn't spend the money. My fear was that he might be able to get enough money in buffalo meat to offset the costs. I couldn't bear to think of it.

I had kept in constant contact with Liz Kellar. I told her that I believed Gary was responsible for Billy's death, and that he neglected his animals. I felt that if the spotlight were fixed on him, his ego could not stand to be perceived as a "bad guy." If he did have The Girls hunted down and killed, he would be confirming it. There was already enough pressure on him to not follow through on his threat. I was also hoping that with his name prominently appearing in the paper, and with his wife's position on the board of an animal rescue group consisting of some committed and quality people, it would prevent him from harming the buffalo girls.

I had just hung up the phone with Liz when there was a call on the other line. The man's voice said, "This is Bill the Slaughterer." It took me a few moments to get my mind around that. He didn't wait for a reply, "I have Gary standing here next to me. He will sell you the buffalo today if you will agree to take on the liability. If you don't agree to it right now, he is hiring me to go shoot and slaughter them."

I couldn't believe how calm I was, "You tell Gary that I will not buy the buffalo, but I will take them."

I heard Bill the Slaughterer talking to Gary. He came back on the line and said, "Gary agrees. Give me your fax number and I will fax over the agreement. I will give you my fax number to fax it right back." I told him I would not be back to my office in Danville until later that evening to review it.

I felt such a relief for a brief moment. But I knew Robert would not agree to accept the liability of buffalo on the loose. I began to call insurance brokers to get insurance, but no one would issue a policy until they were safely contained.

When Robert came home, I showed him the agreement. I reminded him that unfortunately we no longer had any assets to worry about losing. I presented the best case I could to end this traumatic situation with the animals, but Robert would not agree. I felt in my heart that God had given us this gift, this miracle, and that if we trusted in Him it would all work out. I felt so strongly about it, but so did Robert about not taking on that liability. I completely understood. How could I make a unilateral decision that not only defied all logic but would be fundamentally and rationally irresponsible? I agonized about what to do.

I have always been a risk taker, yet I did not feel this was a risk at all. I felt it was The Answer. For the next few days I went back and forth with Robert and within myself, while Gary continued to threaten to shoot The Girls if I didn't sign. Finally I made what was the logical decision to not sign the agreement, knowing in my heart I was denying what God had planned to rescue us all. My hesitation and lack of faith would prove to be a costly mistake in time, money, and heartache. It taught me a valuable lesson. When you ask for God's favor and when he gives it, do not falter. I don't ever want to be ashamed for lack of faith like that again. The consequences prove to be too great.

■ NEWS UPDATE

Owner of missing buffalo: 'We're running out of choices'

BY LIZ KELLAR
Staff Writer

The clock might be running down for a buffalo cow and her 1-year-old calf as they continued to roam free nearly a week after they escaped their pasture on Dog Bar Road.

"There have been no recent sightings," Nevada County Animal Control Officer Falls said Thursday. "The last sighting was Tuesday morning at a pond on Wolf Creek Road and since then, nothing."

As the clock ticks, owner Gary has become concerned with liability issues should the buffalo cause an accident or attack someone.

"Something is going to have be done," he said Thursday. "I'm thinking of having someone hunt them down and put them down. It doesn't appear they're going to be able to be captured, and I'm afraid that if I brought her back, she'd just go through another fence. I regret having to make that decision, but we're running out of choices."

Plans to lure them back to

See BUFFALO A10

BUFFALO:
Continued from A1

the pond with food have proved fruitless so far, Falls said. And the hope of relocating the errant pair to a buffalo ranch on Garden Bar Road has petered out.

Gary said his bull died from parasites two weeks ago.

The rancher is concerned the cow and calf also could be infected with the same parasites, Falls said.

"He doesn't want to disrupt his herd," she added.

There is a slim possibility a zoo might want the animals — but tracking, tranquilizing and transporting the bison is going to be problematic, at best.

"It's going to be a task," Falls said. "We're more than willing to help in any way we can, but we don't have the resources. Our darts probably wouldn't even penetrate their hide.

"It would be nice if they went way back in the forest and were never seen again," Falls said. "It's the perfect environment. There's lot of food out there for them. They'll probably do better through the winter than cattle would."

The two bison, accompanied by a guard donkey, escaped from their enclosure on Dog Bar Road Saturday; the donkey was recaptured after the animals were spotted on Tiger Tail and Buck Ridge roads.

To contact Staff Writer Liz Kellar, e-mail lkellar@theunion.com or call 477-4229.

Trusting in Miracles

Two days later, Gary was on the other end of the phone line, and began with, "I am not the monster you think I am."

I said, "Could you really kill Minko and eat her?"

He was caught off guard and paused a few moments, "Well, I couldn't, but it would be a shame to waste the meat."

Did he think that was better than saying, yes he would eat her? That it would be okay if someone else ate her? That it would be perfectly fine for Billy's sweet little girl to be butchered and sliced up into a medium rare steak on someone's plate, with her bloody juices running onto their green beans?

I said, "Look Gary, why are you thinking about shooting them? You would hire your friend Bill the Slaughterer to hunt them down and shoot them dead. I want to hire someone to track them down and shoot them with a tranq gun so they can live. We would be doing the exact same thing except my way has a better out come." Of course with my way, I realized that Gary wouldn't get any money for those pounds of fresh meat.

He said, "Well you don't have the liability. I do."

I began to reason with the unreasonable, "Think about it now. You have the liability until they are found no matter which one of us hires someone to find them. Once you kill them or I tranq them, you are then relieved of any problems, so why don't you try to help me save them? I want to find them just as badly as you do. Just let me finish this. Let them live."

Gary said, "Well, I can't wait much longer," which meant he hadn't understood a word I said.

Our efforts to find The Girls were put on hold for the next three days due to a very powerful storm. I thought of them huddled together under some 200 year old oak tree for protection. These buffalo were accustomed to being under the shelter of a barn during a bad storm. It wasn't that they needed it with all of their natural protection, but it was that they were used to it. I felt so bad for them as more and more of their old life was disappearing. I could not imagine what they were thinking.

After ten days missing, The Girls and I got an call from a hobby buffalo rancher named Mike, who had read about The Girls' plight in the paper and offered to take them into his herd. He was so sweet on the phone and so concerned about them. He had acreage, the right fencing, and he never used his bison for meat. Once there, The Girls would never have to leave. It was perfect. I thanked him and told him he was the answer to my prayers, and I would call him as soon as we had the buffalo contained.

I hung up the phone, and scooped up my keys to begin my day looking for The Girls. I felt a rush of enthusiasm, knowing I had a wonderful place for them. The phone rang again and it was Liz Kellar asking me what we were going to do now? I said, "Keep on looking. I found a perfect home for them . . ."

Liz interrupted, "Don't you know?"

I said, "Know what?" Liz told me that the buffalo had returned to Gary's property two nights prior during the big storm.

No one could believe they had returned. It was truly a miracle. I felt all along that it was the only way we could ever move the buffalo to safety, but I could not torture myself to think about something that everyone said would never happen.

I sat down relieved that they were at least safe for the moment, and as I began to reflect on all that had transpired, I also began to see answers. I was disappointed in myself that I did not look at the situation through Napini's eyes, because once I did, it made perfect sense that they would return to Billy's Place. I knew that Nappy would have found life in the wilderness hard and foreign. She would not find Billy, and I believe she had a reached the point of resignation in losing him. She knew that if she went back home, her loving Auntie would be there to make sure she was taken care of. We were a family and buffalo need family. With all of my warts and human shortcomings, I was her Auntie who would always be there for her and Minko.

Once again, these buffalo defied what the "experts" had said about them, not understanding the depths of their emotions and intellect. I also denied what I know about them, listening to the common knowledge of ignorance. How could I have done that?

I thanked God for this miracle. I also asked His forgiveness for not trusting Him and not signing the agreement, and for not believing that He would tell The Girls to return to Billy's Place. Had I trusted these things, I would have saved myself all those days of grief and effort that were fruitless and unnecessary.

I reached for the agreement to sign the buffalo over to me. I signed it, got in my car and headed for Billy's Place. Even though Billy was not there, I had renewed joy to see The Girls again. They saw my car and they came a runnin'. They were as happy to see me as I was them . . . well almost.

Napini looked different. She had a resigned look in her eyes. She came right up to the fence and let me hand feed her some carrots, without threatening to gobble up my hand in the process or mock charge me. She even let me pat her face. As I stood there with them, soaking up the joy of it, I said to Nappy, "My God, we have been through a lot together. We girls need to stick together. You know that, don't you? I have a wonderful place for you. I am going to check it out tomorrow if I can, or very soon. We're going to get you out of here. Too many bad memories, and you need a place where you can really be a buffalo. I promised our darling Billy that I would take care of you, and you know I will. That's why you came back. We've had our differences, but I understood why you were angry. All that's in the past. The only thing that matters is I love you, Nappy."

Napini did what she had never done before. She stayed with me and Minko. She wanted to be with her Auntie. It felt good to both of us . . . to the three of us.

As I was leaving, I tacked the signed agreement onto Gary's mailbox so he couldn't miss it.

A Sacramento TV station aired a final story on The Girl's return. In the video, Gary called to Minko and reached for her to come to him. Minko did not make a move, and her eyes said it all. Gary had always complained when Minko came to us because she would never respond to him. She was not about to respond now either. She was not participating in this charade of a caring owner in front of the camera, who just a week before wanted to hunt her down, kill her, and sell her body to a butcher.

I called Mike, the buffalo hobby rancher, to arrange to see his herd and to see this wonderful home for Nappy and Minko. I was delighted to see that his buffalo were healthy and beautiful and so was the property. Mike was caring and responsible and I was thrilled The Girl's would be with his herd. I immediately went home and sent Gary an e-mail that I wanted to pick up the buffalo in a few days, and I placed a call to the hauler who could move them. I kept visualizing Nappy and Minko running with the buffalo at Mike's beautiful ranch, and anticipating that I would soon be able to keep my promise to Billy.

But Gary had other ideas.

I didn't hear from him, so I e-mailed him again and left a message on his voicemail. He did not return my messages, and I began to be concerned. That day, Liz Kellar's latest article appeared about the bison returning home, with Gary quoted as saying he thought he just might keep them now. My heart sank. Gary was going to claim the agreement was not valid. It was not over by a long shot.

Back home on the range
Missing buffalo baby and mom roam home in rainstorm

Photo for The Union by John Hart

A buffalo cow and her calf turned up Wednesday in their home pasture at Gary   property on Dog Bar Road, apparently driven home from their roam by rainy days.

BY LIZ KELLAR
Staff Writer

The buffalo are no longer on the lam. An errant cow and her 1-year-old calf, missing since Oct. 3, returned to owner Gary   property some time during the night Tuesday.

"The storm must have brought them home," said Nevada County Animal Control Officer   Falls. "Gary   left the gate open and this morning, they were there."

The two buffalo escaped from their enclosure on Dog Bar Road a few weeks after the cow's mate died. They were spotted on several occasions near a pond on Buck Ridge Road, but efforts to capture them had proved fruitless.

"They had a good time," Falls said. "They had their walkabout."

The 10-day adventure in the wild does not seem to have done the buffalo any harm, Gary said.

"They look excellent," he said. "The cow seems to be settled down now, she's very tranquil. They're back into their old routine."

Gary had become concerned with liability issues and was contemplating hiring a

> "The storm must have brought them home. Gary left the gate open and this morning, they were there."
>
> — FALLS,
> county animal control officer

tracker to hunt them down. But neighbor (Billy's Auntie), who said she had been helping to care for the animals for the last four and a half months, had not given up on mama Napini and baby Minko.

"I've found a buffalo ranch that called me and told me they would take them," (Auntie) said Wednesday morning.

But Gary   is no longer sure he is interested in surrendering the pair, saying the buffalo ranches he has contacted just want the animals for meat.

"I haven't made up my mind what I'm going to do," he said. "(The cow) hasn't made any attempt at challenging the fences, so I may just keep them."

To contact Staff Writer Liz Kellar, e-mail lkellar@theunion.com or call 477-4229.

Buffalo Extortion

I had been referred to an incredible woman, named Joan Briody, who was a retired attorney. She had been an animal activist, using her legal prowess to advocate for animals for over 40 years. Joan knew it all, had done it all and had seen it all. I had heard from several different animal groups that she was highly regarded, living on an animal advocate pedestal, and that turned out to be completely accurate. The added bonus was, this remarkable lady was living only ten minutes away from us.

I knew I was in for a battle with Gary and needed some legal advice. I was hoping Joan could be of some help, even though she no longer practiced. Joan was not some help, Joan was THE help. When I told her the story of Billy, and Napini and Minko's escape, the agreement, and now Gary not wanting to give up the buffalo, she responded quickly, professionally and with heart to save those buffalo girls. It was as if I had known her all my life, she was my best friend, and those buffalo were her family too.

Joan advised me to send Gary a registered letter informing him that I was going to pick up the animals on Saturday at 1 pm, and to please acknowledge that he had received it. We would be accompanied by the hauler and would need access to his gate to retrieve the buffalo.

On Friday evening, Gary e-mailed that we should come on over, along with a veiled threat and some choicer words that meant we were in for another confrontation.

Joan advised that we call the Sheriff and ask an officer to meet us there to avoid any trouble. Joan said to bring the agreement to show the deputies my rightful ownership of the buffalo. I called the sheriff's department dispatch and was told that they would not send someone out unless there was a problem. They did not have the time or resources to oblige my request to avoid a problem. I told them to stand by because there would be.

We arrived a few minutes before the stated time and parked along the street to wait for Joe the hauler. Joe had taken Billy to his necropsy, and he handled him respectfully, keeping my ribbon and the picture of Billy and me where I had placed them. He knew how much those buffalo meant to me.

While Robert and I were waiting anxiously inside the truck for Joe, a vehicle pulled into Gary's driveway with signage that read, BEAR RIVER SLAUGHTER. We both gasped, and Robert jumped out of the truck and ran full speed toward the slaughter truck. Gary and The Clan had

gathered behind the security of their locked gate at the end of the driveway. I grabbed the cell phone, barely able to punch in the numbers from
shaking, and called the sheriff. I said, " I told you there would be a problem and there is!" I saw Robert was in a heated conversation with Bill the
Slaughterer. I continued, "We are involved in an altercation with a slaughterer and our buffalo. HELP!"

Then I hung up and called Liz Kellar. I could barely speak I was so
out of breath, not from exercise, but out of sheer terror, "Liz, you have
to come. Gary has a slaughterer here! I am so scared he will hurt those
girls. PLEASE COME! "Liz said she was on her way.

Then I called Joan in the same oxygen-starved voice, "Joan, a slaughterer is here! I called the sheriff. What do I do?" Joan's voice was equally
as panicked. She asked me if the slaughter was imminent. I said, "No,
because Robert was still talking to the guy in the driveway." Robert now
appeared more angry than frightened.

Joan said, "When the sheriff comes, show them your ownership agreement and tell them to stay there to make sure you can move them without
provocation or harm coming to the animals." I thanked her and said I'd
call her back. Then I called Mike and told him the story and that we might
not be able to get the buffalo to his ranch that day. Mike was so kind and
concerned and said not to worry.

During this whole scene, The Girls and Whiskey were standing at the
fence waiting for us. I was so glad they couldn't read the words on that truck.

Three sheriff's cars arrived within minutes. I guess they weren't that
busy after all. Joe also pulled up with his trailer, and Robert told him to
wait in his truck. Gary and The Clan, with their good friend Bud Weiser
obviously involved, were still safely behind the locked gate laughing at our
panic and yelling something about having bison burgers for dinner.

Bill the Slaughterer, who I referred to as BS for short, approached the
deputies, and they huddled around to talk. Meanwhile, Robert told me
that BS said that if we paid Gary $4000 for the buffalo we could have
them, otherwise he was there to slaughter them right in front of us. Robert
warned him that the sheriff was coming, and that he had better not be
a part of any illegal act against our buffalo. BS was actually a friend of
Gary's, and he argued that the agreement wasn't valid because I did not
sign it on the day he sent it, and it had been rescinded.

After about 15 minutes with BS talking alone with the deputies, with
Gary and The Clan not making a move from behind the gate, the officers

looked like they might walk off. I jumped out of the truck and yelled, "Officers! Can we speak to you now?"

One officer, who I assumed was in charge said, "What for?"

I said, "What for?" You need to hear our side." He started to walk away. I said, "Officer, we need to speak to you. We are here to pick up our buffalo and this man told us he will slaughter them unless we pay $4000. Isn't that extortion?"

Evidently extortion is not considered a crime in Nevada County because they did not seem interested. BS denied he told Robert he was going to slaughter the buffalo if we didn't pay. He stated he was just there as a friend to Gary.

I said to the officer, "I just hung up from my attorney. She told us to show you the written agreement, and that you should be here to make sure we can get the buffalo moved safely. There is our hauler waiting."

The words "extortion," "slaughter," and "written agreement," as well as our obvious distress, meant nothing to this peace officer. The word "attorney" was what finally grabbed his attention. The officer stopped and asked for the agreement, and BS interrupted reiterating that the agreement was not valid. I could see the deer in the headlights look on the officer's face, as he was trying to figure out what to do. It was clear that he really didn't want to do anything but get back in his patrol car and be busy. My main concern was that Gary not harm the animals. At this point, I did not know what he was capable of, especially when he had the support of the whole Clan there, and Bud Weiser.

I could see I was not going to get any real action out of the confused deputy, so I switched gears. "This is a civil matter and it has got to be decided in court. Therefore, will you please advise Gary that he better not harm those animals until we have a judge decide ownership."

That was an easy discussion for the deputy that wouldn't involve a lot of delay in leaving, so he walked down the driveway, and up to the gate where Gary and The Clan had taken their positions. They talked for a while and the officer returned saying, "Gary says you feed these animals, which is trespassing, so you can't do it anymore."

I said, "Explain trespassing and not being able to feed my own animals?" He explained that we could stand at the fence because that was county property, but if we put our hands over the fence, or threw food into the pasture, that would be trespassing. I explained that Gary had never fed the animals properly, and how Billy had died.

The officer smugly looked over at the buffalo and said, "Well they look pretty healthy to me."

I said, "Only because we fed them." The officer acted like we were just nuisances interrupting his day.

He added. "Gary says if his animals end up dead it, will be because you fed them and poisoned them."

I said, "Oh my God. We love these animals and would never do them any harm. I consider this a threat, and I am very concerned that he will harm them and blame us. Please tell him that we promise not to feed the animals anymore, but that he has to take good care of them until this is decided in court." I looked over at the three Kids still waiting for us at the fence, and my heart sank.

While I was talking to the officers, Bill the Slaughterer was talking privately to Robert. BS told him that if we went to court it would cost us $4000 in legal fees, and we wouldn't win anyway. So he suggested we make Gary an offer, and "all this will go away." It was clear they had hatched this extortion plot with a lot of thought, and I'm sure, with a great deal of satisfaction.

The officer returned to say he had warned Gary not to harm the animals as I had suggested. Robert pointed out to BS that Gary was not much of a friend to him. Gary was potentially involving him in a legal dispute. If he shot and slaughtered the buffalo, and the judge later determined they were ours, BS would be liable.

The sheriffs deputy confirmed that was true. BS was real quiet after that. The only thing he said was, "Just make Gary an offer and all this will be over."

First of all, we didn't have $4000, not even half that. Robert and I conferred, and we told Bill the Slaughterer that we would e-mail Gary that evening.

Before we left, we looked over to the pasture, and The Kids were still waiting for us by the fence. I said to the officer, "Who do you think these animals want to be with?" He looked over and acted surprised, as if maybe what we were telling them was true after all. It made us feel terrible that we could not go over and give them treats and be with them, especially after they had waited so patiently and faithfully. As we drove off, I made the mistake of turning back to see The Kids watching us drive out of their lives for the next few months. Our emotions hit rock bottom.

Liz Kellar's article appeared the next day. Gary stated that he was never going to harm the buffalo and that BS was only there to show his support. Gary's brother stated that they were going to consult with their Choctaw Nation about how to proceed. I pictured an entire ancestral Choctaw Nation turning over in their graves that one of their own would use their sacred buffalo as pawns for money and to hurt someone who had cared so deeply for them.

After talking to Joan for guidance, we e-mailed Gary and offered him $1100. That was a fair price at the time for a six year old bison and her baby. That also was all the money we had. If we would have had $10,000 we would have paid it. A condition of the sale was that it included Whiskey. Even though he was priceless to us, as Jack Arnold had said, in this economy people couldn't give away their horses, what's more a Jack donkey.

Gary never replied.

Not being able to take care of The Kids was heart wrenching. After the escape, Napini had made the decision to return to our care, and now we were abandoning her. We felt Gary was not going to ever take responsibility for their proper care, and we feared their health would again be in jeopardy. Thank God I had dewormed them the week before so they would be safe from parasites for another three months. Robert and I discussed the dilemma we faced. Should we go visit The Kids without feeding them or being able to touch them? We knew how difficult it would be to go there and have Gary and The Clan screaming at us and upsetting the animals. They wouldn't understand the turmoil, and how could we just stand at the fence without performing our normal ritual of being food servers and donkey masseuses?

We made the painful decision not to go see them. The Kids would not understand why we would seem so distant, and it would seem mean of us to just stand there and not feed or be able to interact with them. But the most important reason was, that we feared if we kept showing up and aggravating Gary, it would give him the excuse and opportunity to harm them and say we did it. If someone were capable of killing and slaughtering his "pets," we had to err on the side of caution. It felt like we were severing our own body parts to sever ourselves away from The Kids, but we could not take the chance that they might otherwise pay the price. I just prayed that Billy would whisper to them that we did not abandon them. They would have to muster all their buffalo patience and wait for us to come for them.

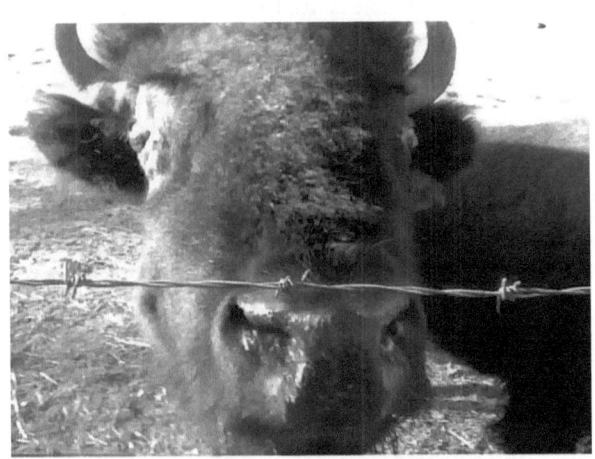

How sad it was that Napini and Minko were waiting for us at the fence; but instead, we had to drive away not knowing when we would see them again.

Gary's Poison Pen Letter

After the newspaper articles appeared stating Gary was thinking about shooting The Girls, and along with my accusations of neglect, Gary was getting a public relations pounding. While Liz Kellar was more than fair in reporting the story, it was clear enough that Gary was no PETA member. He had not liked the articles' portrayal of him, and he had threatened to sue the paper.

They agreed to publish his letter with his explanation about the situation:

Well Cared For Buffaloes Don't Need Saving

Six years ago I purchased two buffalo calves as pets. The bull was named Bill and the cow, Napini, a Choctaw name my Choctaw mother chose. I chose these animals as pets because of my heritage. It was a tremendous pleasure for my family, friends and I to watch them grow.

On Sept. 5, 2008, they surprised us with a beautiful calf born on my cousin's birthday who had just passed away from a heart attack. His name was Duke. In memory of him, she was named Minko, which means "Duke" in Choctaw. Soon after, I purchased the donkey, Whiskey, a rescue, from my friends, Bill and Katie Gonzales. They all became a happy family.

My pets were always a favorite attraction for visiting friends and relatives. Many pictures and stories went to China, Morocco, Brazil and numerous parts of the U.S.

My animals have always had the space, food, water, shelter and love they need and deserve. Many can attest to that.

A few months ago, I noticed a woman almost daily, parked at my fence. She was feeding and talking to my animals for two to three hours every visit. I didn't pay too much attention as they'd always drawn many spectators.

It soon became obvious that she was obsessed with the buffalo and donkey. Soon, her husband seemed to be just as involved and they were using my barn and facilities as if they owned them.

I never knew when they were there or not. They seemed to believe they could come and go as they wished. I don't have a clear view of the barn from my house.

I have had these animals, healthy and content for six years.

There was never a problem until they fed them strawberries, melons, apples and other things they hadn't eaten before. Once the bull showed signs of distress, a vet dewormed all of them. Unfortunately, by then it was too late for Bill. There was already too much damage.

When Bill died, Napini started acting strangely and aggressively. She started tearing up things in and around the barn. I was hoping it would pass but it didn't.

I awoke on a Saturday morning to a horn honking at my gate. The gentleman told me my buffalo were loose. I followed him to where they'd been seen last. After a fruitless search I returned home to see how they escaped. The cow had ripped through two fences. She was determined to find her mate.

The three - Napini, Minko and Whiskey - eventually entered an enclosed yard and I thought we had them, but Napini was not going to be contained, and she and the calf bolted through the driveway gate. Whiskey opted to stay. The people around Tiger Tail and Buck Ridge were fantastic during this ordeal.

After a number of days, I stated the animals might have to be put down as a last resort. These weren't two Yorkie terriers on a stampede. These animals can easily kill a human.

As the days passed, I grew more and more concerned about liability. When (The Woman) heard that I may have to put them down, she frantically called and said she would accept responsibility that day.

An agreement was sent to her via fax, to be signed and returned by 5 pm that day. She wasn't heard from again until my buffalo returned home.

She wouldn't accept any responsibility when they were at risk, but as soon as they were safely confined, where they're now content, she claims ownership.

My wife is an officer on the board of directors of an animal rescue group. We've saved three animals ourselves. I volunteer 20 to 25 hours per week at Hospice. Do we sound like we would abuse our pets?

Gary _____ lives in Grass Valley.

In the article, Gary pretended not to know me. I was the Obsessed Buffalo Stalker Auntie. The truth was, for four and a half months, Gary and I night-owled almost 80 e-mails to each other consisting of me telling him what adorable things his animals were doing . . . especially Billy, and all about their care and progress. I also wrote the article about him and the buffalo, had a party for him and saw him regularly while feeding his animals. What's more, Gary specifically left Billy in my care the weekend he died.

I could only access the barn if I had the combination to open the security gate. Obviously he had given me the combination.

His rationale that because he volunteered at the Hospice Thrift Shop and "saved" some animals, (I doubt Billy and the Kids would vouch for that) he couldn't be an abuser. Since Hospice is one of the most respected and worthwhile organizations, it's too bad he didn't think of the Hospice style of compassionate care for Billy and The Kids while he was busy feather dusting trinkets in the store. And it's too bad his estranged wife didn't bother to check up on Billy, since she was on the board of an animal rescue group.

Of course, we all know melons and berry treats will kill an animal, although veterinarians obviously don't since they were advising every step of the way.

The parasite killers do not come from produce but from feces. Nothing was mentioned about the hay and feeds that were the real staple of their diets, the fact that they were skeletons when I arrived, and the veterinary care I provided.

Both Jack Arnold and Dr. Woodbury predicted I would get used and burned by someone who would neglect his animals - but I didn't feel used. I felt unappreciated for sure, but you can not use someone who gives fully and freely with no expectations or strings attached.

Just like the Choctaw Nation, Billy would be turning over in his grave with this article, if he would have had a grave. Instead Billy's poor emaciated body was carved up into pieces and chunks of specimen tissue that were later insignificantly tossed into an incinerator. But it didn't matter. His precious spirit no longer needed that ravaged body.

My phone rang off the hook the day Gary's article appeared. I was furious of course, but in a way it was also freeing. There was no longer any doubt about the kind of person Gary really was, which made it easier to do what I had to do to protect Billy's girls.

Mitzi Phillips was a well known animal advocate and activist who decided to retire that passionate involvement when she and her husband moved to Grass Valley to lead a quieter life. But when she read the articles in the paper about the buffalo's escape, she called me, offering to help. After reading Gary's poison pen letter she was livid and suggested we get together and write a response. Since Mitzi was an excellent writer, I was flattered and was eager to get her input. However, before we finished our Pulitzer Prize Winning Repudiation, Joan Briody advised against publishing a response. That made no sense to Mitzi or me to let him get away with what he had said and it cut me to the quick to not do any damage control. However, I followed Joan's advice. After all, I was getting free advice from a 40 year retired veteran of animal related legal wars because she genuinely cared. Nappy, Minko and I were so fortunate to have these sincere and powerful women in our corner.

We had neighbors, strangers and people from all walks of life offering to help. The support was overwhelming and appreciated, and gave us a lot of strength both within ourselves and in numbers. A flood of people were calling and e-mailing the Sheriff, who was the head of Animal Control, as well as the District Attorney and the editor of the paper, to voice their concern over the welfare of the buffalo girls and to ask for an investigation into Billy's death. Letters to the editor were published, and a cartoon appeared in the paper showing Napini and Minko Trick or Treating. National and global organizations like Peta, In Defense of Animals, the Humane Society and Action for Animals expressed their concern, but still, no word from the Sheriff. There was not even an acknowledgment of the issue or any kind of response to the requests from the public.

The Attorney with Buffalo Clients

As our financial situation continued to plummet, so did my hope for Napini and Minko. I had no other avenues to pursue. I took a buffalo leap of faith and opened the phonebook to the attorney section. After speaking with four different ones, they all told me what I already knew: my legal position with The Girls was tenuous, at best. The agreement that Gary and I signed was somewhere between a contract and a gift, each posing a nebulous definition and outcome. Unfortunately, the law does not have to be moral, nor is it required to decide what is right.

Every attorney I spoke to wanted a retainer of $4000 to take the case. One of the attorneys had followed the saga in the newspaper and really seemed to care about my situation. He advised me to rally the community support I had received to raise the $4000 to buy the bison from Gary. That was a great idea, but I knew Gary. If the community organized, he would consider it an attack on his character that people wanted to get the buffalo away from him, siding with me, and he would refuse to sell them at any cost. All I could do was pray and try again tomorrow.

The next day, I reached for the phone book again to call more attorneys, summoning my courage to face more rejection. After practicing my appeal four times the day before, I could recite it clearly and concisely. I just could not bring myself to hear the same hopeless responses.

My eyes focused on an ad from an attorney who specialized in animal issues. It was the only ad mentioning animals. My hope perked up, and I called Mary Pollansky-Gravatt and left a message. A few hours later she returned the call and asked how she could help. I explained the situation in a cell phone condensed version, and she immediately advised me to file in small claims court. She explained that it would not cost me much, there was a slim chance I might prevail, or Gary might decide it wasn't worth his time and effort and hand The Girls over. Mary was genuinely concerned, assertive, and immediately emotionally connected. I was so impressed with her and said I would follow her advice, and thanked her profusely.

I filed the lawsuit for ownership of the buffalo in small claims court, and Gary was served. However, the judge dismissed the case, saying it needed to be filed in civil court. If Gary were present that day in court, I didn't see him. It didn't matter that the case didn't go anywhere because it was the first legal step in showing Gary that I was dead serious. He should have known by then how much I loved those girls, and that I was not going to give up.

I called Mary, told her about the ruling, and we agreed to meet in her office the following day. Mary proved to be professional and had a "tell it like it is" personality. She could handle my strong convictions and passion, and harness them in a way that would be most productive. After speaking with her the first time, I knew that Mary was a buffalo attorney before she did.

When she began to explain her fees, I was ready to cover my ears. . . until she said she would not charge me a retainer. She would even give me a reduced rate but said firmly, "I expect when I bill you, that I will be paid right away." Then she chuckled, "I say that to all my clients and it rarely happens."

I told her that I was very grateful and that I would be one of her exceptions. I had no idea how I was going to pay her fees, but I would sell everything I owned if I had to, to keep my side of the bargain. Mary was the miracle I had prayed for, and I trusted that God wouldn't grant a miracle to later become a bad debt. I had faith that business would improve, and the money would come.

Hope had returned. I was reenergized and ready to go to battle for The Girls. I went home and collected all of the e-mails and documentation Mary would need for the case. I put it in a binder and labeled each section. I catalogued and highlighted all of the most important points. The binder was 3 inches thick with evidence of everything that had transpired since the first day I met Billy. I had about 80 e-mails with Gary and about 40 e-mails with Dr. Mario alone. When I handed Mary the binder, she looked in amazement and said. "I wish all my clients were like this. What a paper trail!"

If Mary had any doubt about my love and commitment to the buffalo, the binder took care of it. On the cover of the binder I placed the sweetest picture, my favorite picture of Billy and me. Upon opening the binder, the first page was the message I wrote the day that Billy died. I wanted Mary to be very clear about what this lawsuit was all about and how much it meant.

Mary filed our lawsuit in civil court for ownership of the buffalo, and she served Gary herself to "get a good look at him to size him up." I told her that I was certain he would relinquish The Girls as soon as it affected his wallet. In the meantime, we needed to keep the pressure on him from all sides. If the media continued to cover the story, with the accusations of animal neglect, logic would say he would take care of The Girls. If Animal Control was caught in the crossfire, they would want to make sure of it. Gary thought of himself as a "good ol' boy," and he would not want to tarnish that image.

My Love Affair with Buffalo Billy

Counting the Days to Retirement

I had sent Officer Falls an e-mail, explaining that the last time I was in Gary's barn he had only two bales of hay that had been there for weeks. I had been bringing the feed every day and watching to see if any hay was taken from the barn to determine if he was feeding them. When those bales of hay did not leave the barn, I had decided, before Billy passed away, to talk to animal control to plead for their help.

I asked Falls to please check to see if the bales were still there, which would mean The Girls and Whiskey had not been fed. Robert and I had spoken to her at length the day Billy died, and with my visit to Fevenger, she knew there were allegations of animal neglect. She also saw poor Billy. I was surprised that I did not receive a response so I e-mailed again, but still no reply. Calling Animal Control meant you would leave a message and hope for a returned call, and since I knew the officers were connected to their computers, an e-mail would also leave a record. I e-mailed again, perplexed at not receiving a response from Falls.

There were some neighbors at Billy's Place who had originally seen me feeding the animals and stopped at the fence from time to time. They had even generously brought a bale of alfalfa for The Kids. These neighbors, Julie and James, were kind enough now to keep an eye out for the buffalo and Whiskey, to make sure they were being fed and cared for. Julie called me during this time and told me she hadn't seen evidence that the animals were being fed for a couple of days, and she thought what had previously been put out for them was just straw. I e-mailed Falls my concern and contacted Mary. Again, Falls would not respond to me, so Mary called and left an urgent message. Falls finally returned her call and told Mary that she had been out to the property, looked at the bison from the street, and determined they were "fine." Mary asked her to please be more thorough and perform a welfare check on the buffalo, take a closer look at their condition, and determine if there was food in the barn, and water in the tub. Falls responded that she would have to get Gary's permission to go on his property, and she wasn't about to do it. She also said that if she had any more complaints about the bison's well-being, she would consider it harassment.

It was now very clear that even if the animals were sick, starving to death, or injured, Falls didn't want to know about it. As far as she was concerned they were four letter' 'fine."

When she came to Billy's Place the day he died, she asked to speak to me. I did not want to leave Billy, but I obliged her request. I courteously asked her how she became an animal control officer. I had watched many *Animal Cops* episodes on Animal Planet and naively thought she would respond by explaining her love for animals. Instead she told me that she had a retirement income from Pac Bell, and she was looking for another retirement income. So she applied for the job. Her blunt demeanor shocked me. I mentioned something about how difficult the job must be seeing animals suffer, but her response was even more outrageous. She said that many times she would have to go out and "blow the brains out of Bambi" and she laughed as she mimicked doing it. It wasn't a nervous or embarrassed kind of laughter. I was startled and repulsed by her insensitivity, and especially at a time when I was struggling to save Billy. I quickly excused myself to return to him. I should have known from that conversation what to expect from Falls.

To this day I do not know what happened from the day Billy died, when she promised she would pursue the circumstances of his death, to just a week later when it became clear that she was protecting Gary, not the animals. Falls made no attempt to even get a copy of Billy's necropsy (autopsy).

Mary received no better response from Fevenger, who had essentially turned his management reins over to Falls. Why would Fevenger want to be mired down in management when he also had retirement to think about?

In the meantime, I thought of another angle that might work to get The Girls off Gary's property. I did some research with the county to make sure Gary had the proper zoning to keep buffalo, and if so, that he was in compliance. While he had agricultural zoning, he did not have a permit to keep wild animals and according to the regulations in California, it was no surprise that he did not have adequate fencing for bison. I made a visit to the county zoning department to plead the case. They called Animal Control to determine if the buffalo were considered wild or domestic, and unfortunately Falls intercepted the call and said she had inspected the fencing, and it was adequate. Falls knew nothing about what was necessary to contain bison and obviously did not bother to find out. They had already escaped from that flimsy fence and could easily do it again, as Gary had admitted in one of the newspaper articles. She also declared the animals were livestock, so Gary didn't need a permit. Case closed.

To Falls, the truth was just an irritating and easily dismissible moot point. While I was frustrated again by Animal-Out-of-Control, I knew that another message had been sent to Gary that I would never give up. I knew however, that he would, if money could just hold out that long.

Mary was equally as frustrated by the situation. In the beginning, I had warned her about Animal Control, but she had given them the benefit of the doubt. Now she said, "Time to go higher up" and arranged an appointment with Fevenger's boss, Captain Powell, to insist that they obtain a copy of the necropsy.

As soon as Powell and Fevenger chose their seats for the meeting and sat down, I knew the meeting was over. Powell sat as far from Mary and I as he possibly could, and he even crossed his arms in front of his chest. If he had taken a course in body language and customer relations I am sure he must have flunked it. Mary explained that we needed Animal Control to do a thorough investigation into Billy's death.

Powell blurted it out, the unbelievable and irrefutable truth that no one in the entire department knew what they were talking about, what Falls was up to, nor did they care. He said, "Well as I understand it, the bull died of parasites." I cringed to hear Billy referred to so impersonally as "the bull". And with that comment, Powell thought the meeting should be over. He and Fevenger could go back to their offices and plan their old age outings.

Since Mary was sitting there momentarily dumbfounded by Powell's ineptitude, I responded to his statement, "Yes, that is absolutely right. The necropsy stated he died from parasites and nutritional deficiency." Powell had thought he had rested his case, so he did not know what to say. Wisely, he remained silent.

Watching your animal starve to death and doing nothing about it is a crime. Letting an animal be eaten alive from the inside is immoral. Not doing anything about this suffering is an injustice. There is a greater judgment than from Nevada County Animal Control.

After Mary continued to press Powell to act, he finally and reluctantly agreed to have an investigation into Billy's death, and he promised that the process would include interviewing me and seeing the evidence I had to support the animal neglect claim. We stressed that there were still 2 buffalo and a donkey on the property, about whose well-being we were concerned. Mary also told him that a lawsuit had been filed against Gary for ownership of the buffalo. She wanted Powell and Fevenger to know we meant business.

A week passed and I did not hear from anyone at Animal Control. I called Mary to find out if she had heard from anyone but she had not. I asked Mary to send Fevenger a few critical documents to start the report. Mary complied and explained that they could review all of the documentation when they met with me. Even though we had Powell's promise that Animal Control would contact me, we were beginning to be skeptical of his word. What we did not know was that they had given the responsibility to Falls to do the report and she had been working on it. We were under the impression from the meeting with Powell that Fevenger would do the report. Had we any idea Falls would be assigned to it, we would have stipulated that Fevenger himself complete it. But what would it have mattered anyway, since Powell's word, the word of a Captain in law enforcement, proved to mean nothing?

To be fair, I am sure there must have been some good and conscientious people working in law enforcement for this county, but none that we dealt with. It is up to us, the people, to step up and change things in government, or we eventually suffer for that which we have settled.

Napini and Minko's Day in Court

After six agonizing weeks of not seeing The Girls, the first hearing arrived. I had petitioned the court to order a monitor for the buffalo's health and safety while awaiting the trial, which would be about three months away. I wanted to make sure they were being well cared for. It was also my hope that it might encourage Gary to give them up. A court appointed monitor would be there looking over his shoulder to make sure he was diligent with their food and water and that their stall would be cleaned. Gary would hate any form of accountability, and he would finally be forced to step up to the plate.

Since Mary told me I did not have to be at the hearing, I scheduled a client's living room installation that day in the Bay area so I would be able to pay Mary's bill right away. However, the judge asked both parties to go immediately into mediation. Mary called me and asked if I were available to do this by phone. I said I could, and I instructed my installation crew what to do for the next hour and waited for Mary to call me from the meeting.

Mary started the mediation by saying that we wanted to make certain the animals were being taken care of properly for the next three months, since I was not allowed on the property to feed them or verify their well-being. Gary argued that his animals were never neglected, and there was no reason for it. He said he had the evidence to prove it, and he handed some papers to the mediator saying, "This is a report from Animal Control stating there was no neglect in my bull's death."

Even over the phone, I could hear Mary fly out of her seat as she grabbed the report. She was furious that he and Falls had blindsided us. Mary said, "When did you get this?"

Gary just couldn't help put his foot in his mouth as he said proudly, "I picked it up from Officer Falls yesterday."

I was shrieking into the phone but no one could hear me. Gary and Falls thought they had struck the lethal blow. But Mary was too smart for them and said, "I have not been privy to this "evidence", as you put it, and I doubt its validity. This report has no bearing whatsoever on this meeting anyway, because we are not here to determine if Billy died from neglect. Our lawsuit isn't about Billy. It's about the rightful ownership of the two female bison based on a signed agreement, and making sure they are properly taken care of pending the trial date. My client is the owner of these buffalo, and she is not allowed to be on the property to take care of them. Therefore a monitor needs to be assigned to be sure that they are."

Good work, Mary. I knew she was just as upset as I was over the report, and she was trying to mask it. Falls and Gary planned that he would have the report for this meeting and we would know nothing about it. However, their collusion to derail this motion had failed, as Mary directed the mediator back to our reason to mediate. This set the tone for a vitriolic two hours. Frustrated and confused, Gary finally agreed to allow a third party monitor, that I would pay for, to visit his property once a week to see that The Girls had adequate food and water and that their stall was clean. Gary's last snarl was, "I suppose she wants me to bring them a pillow and a blanket too!"

The judge signed off on the agreement to make it binding. I told Mary to tell Gary, "Thank you" and I really meant it. She didn't tell me his reply.

Mary and I couldn't believe Gary had agreed to this because he didn't have to. As I saw it, he agreed for three reasons. First, the mediator stressed that if we did not come up with an agreement, the judge would decide. The judge was never going to make the ruling that I could go on Gary's property to take care of the buffalo, and he probably would have ruled to have a monitor do it. The natural choice for a court appointed monitor would have been Animal Control, which would have meant that Gary would have been able to do whatever he wanted with Falls in his corner. He should have let the judge decide, as it could not have turned out any worse for him than what he agreed to in mediation. Secondly, he was so concerned about having his image tarnished as an animal abuser, that he painted himself into a corner. If he did not agree to have the animals monitored, it would have appeared he had something to hide. And last but not least, Gary knew I would never give up.

I was so happy that I could take back some control over The Girl's welfare. But now I needed to find a monitor . . . a very cheap monitor. And it was bad timing being so close to Christmas. I also dreaded more volatility coming from Gary, which was certain to happen with the court now looking over his shoulder.

Just One Dead Buffalo

Billy's necropsy stated that he died from parasites and nutritional deficiency, although there were no parasites present. The absence of parasites was explained by the deworming that had taken place a couple of months before he died. But by then it was too late. The parasites had done too much damage. All of my care and feeding couldn't have saved him. We had been searching all those months for some kind of illness or disease that we could cure, never thinking he would die from something so cruelly simple and so easily preventable.

After reviewing the necropsy and supposedly speaking to the vet who performed it, Falls concluded in her official report that buffalo commonly get parasites or worms, and they can die from them. She stated in her report that she asked the vet who performed the necropsy if it showed Billy died from neglect, and the vet said, "Absolutely not." She stated that if I had seen the buffalo starving, why had I not contacted Animal Control to report it? She said that I might have caused the parasites by feeding the animals. However, the ultimate insult was that she spelled Billy's name as Billee. She never read any of the documentation that Mary sent, or she would have known how to spell my darling's name. She could have at least done that right.

It was a ridiculous and completely biased report. The necropsy identified the type of parasite, which is from larvae that come from feces. Had Falls bothered to find that out, she would have known she could not accuse me of feeding the buffalo parasites. Saying that buffalo can get worms and can die from them is like saying kids can get the flu and they can die from it. If a child gets the flu, his condition worsens, his temperature gets over 102 degrees and nothing is done to help the child except watch it die, that parent would be charged with neglect. Especially if there were a history that they were told what to do by a doctor and they ignored it. Or in simpler terms, if a child got an intestinal parasite and nothing was done, while the parents watched the child grow weaker, losing 1/2 of his body weight and finally die, those parents would end up in prison. It was the same situation with Billy, except it was more heinous. Billy's cure was an over the counter remedy. All Gary had to do was ask someone half way knowledgeable about livestock or farm animals losing weight. If he didn't want to pay for a vet, he could have asked someone at the feed store, found a local rancher, gone online to buffalo websites or buffalo ranch websites. Anyone of these would have first recommended deworming Billy for his symptoms. How could he sit by and watch his "pet" continue to lose weight and finally starve to death?

Billy's parasites came from that disgustingly filthy place that was never cleaned up. Not only did Gary not treat him, he barely fed him, which contributed to his fatal nutritional deficiency. Dr. Woodbury had been correct when he suggested that Billy might be severely copper deficient. I believe Gary killed Billy just as sure as a bullet to the head, except that would have been more humane.

The necropsy substantiated what caused Billy's death. It did not substantiate if his death was caused by neglect. No competent veterinarian would have done an autopsy of an animal's starvation from parasites and nutritional deficiency and then say he "Absolutely was not" a victim of neglect.

If an autopsy was done on a child who starved to death, the autopsy would say the cause of death, and it would be up to law enforcement to gather the evidence and then for the prosecutor to file charges based on the evidence. I had a three inch thick binder of evidence to point out the truth: documentation of weekly e-mails from/to Gary, e-mails to the vets, vet bills with instructions for Gary to properly care for his animals, communication from bison experts, my feed bills, and the emaciated photos of Billy and The Kids when I met them. Falls could have spoken directly to any of these experts, and had she taken the time to do a thorough investigation, she should have determined that Gary neglected his animals before and after I met him.

In my view, Nevada County Animal Control didn't care about the truth or the law. It was all about doing as little as possible and distorting the facts to justify it.

Not only was Fall's report full of factual errors and omissions, it was an official document containing grammatical and spelling errors. It was a hastily written report designed to sweep the whole issue under the carpet. If a report were going to be stone walled, why bother to do spell check? To this animal welfare public servant, what did the life of one buffalo matter anyway? Why spend any time on it at all …. especially when there was retirement to think about.

The Choice

The course of our lives is determined by our choices. We either gather our strength and choose to do the right things or we choose to be weak. It really all boils down to that.

Each choice we make not only affects our lives but the lives of others. If we make a decision based on emotion or passion, sometimes it can catapult us to a new level of accomplishment. Yet emotion without proper perspective can also lead us in unproductive directions.

Since we cannot fight every battle, our decisions as to which conflicts to tackle need to be based on which ones will lead us to accomplish our goals. If a battle will divert us away from our dreams, our goals, our destiny, then we know we have to walk away from it and leave it to the One who will handle it for us. Sometimes, walking away from the battle or ignoring the opposition is the ultimate strength, not to mention the ultimate wisdom.

I was now faced with a very important choice. Should I spend the time and effort to get justice for Billy? It seemed so wrong not to hold Gary and Animal Control accountable. But the facts were clear; as much as my love and devotion to Billy wanted to engage that battle, even if I obtained the justice he deserved, it wouldn't bring my boy back, nor would it accomplish taking care of The Girls. So I chose to focus my efforts in a completely positive direction. I chose to make sure I kept my promise this time, which meant I would have to leave justice and judgment in the hands of the Ultimate Judge. Perhaps later I could pursue changing the culture at Animal Control and to turn the District Attorney's attention to prosecuting these cases.

Still, that didn't mean I could let go that easily. My anger would regularly rear its ugly head at the injustice of all that had happened. In order to make it easier to let it go and stay focused on my promise to take care of The Girls, I developed this picture in my mind:

Gary, Fevenger, Powell, Falls, and the Sheriff arrive on the exact same day at the Pearly Gates. They are surprised to see each other and begin to celebrate, until they happen to look over to the other side of the gates. They see God sitting on his celestial throne, with Billy lying majestically at His feet. God is lovingly stroking Billy's fluffy bangs and says, "Well, look who's here. You all remember my boy, Billy, don't you?"

My Love Affair with Buffalo Billy

The Christmas Gift

I had waged a battle for The Girls using every tactic I could. Something had to work. Gary was within days of having to answer the lawsuit ,and he would have to hire an attorney. My biggest gamble, that Gary wouldn't spend any money on attorney's fees to keep The Girls he had been so willing to shoot and slaughter, was about to reach the moment of truth. So were our dwindling finances. We had spent about $3800 in attorney's fees and we hadn't yet gone to trial.

Christmas was swiftly approaching. The year before, on Christmas day, I had read RD Rosen's book about Roger Brooks' bonded and loving relationship with his buffalo, Charlie, that I had always dreamed of having. Within six months I had my special bond with Billy. But I had tragically lost that brief dream-come-true, and now I was fighting for Napini and Minko. There was no doubt in my mind that if they stayed at the Concentration Camp, they would end up like Billy. . . dead.

It was around 1 pm and I was looking somberly out of the window at the dreary sky and the lifeless rain, but there was comfort in knowing the rain would bring a bright green carpet of grass. Nature would provide something for the buffalo girls and Whiskey to eat, even though parasites were a constant threat from eating off the ground. I envisioned the buffalo girls huddled under the big oak tree for shelter, or just standing in the rain, defying it with their beautiful new winter coats. Or maybe they were bedded down in the barn together. Then, I thought of them lying in a barn not having been cleaned for two months.

The phone interrupted that angry thought, and I answered it without enthusiasm.

"Hi, it's Mary Polansky-Gravatt."

I responded with a question, "Mary?"

She said, "I just got a call from Gary. You can have The Girls, and he wants you to come get them as soon as possible."

Life can change forever in small surprising moments. I felt a calm wave of relief; then a split second of doubt shadowed over me that it could be true. When Mary confirmed that it was indeed true, I felt overwhelming gratitude that The Girls were finally safe, and I was able to ensure their future. I burst into joyful and humble tears. All of the strength I had mustered over the last several months seemed not to need me anymore, and I was glad to say goodbye to the strain of it.

However, I was naive to think that the ordeal was over. It would take another two months to get the buffalo girls off the property, and the agony of dealing with Gary and his Clan was only going to get worse. Very soon I was going to have to invite that strength back and ask it to bring more troops.

Adventures in Moving

All of my attention was now directed toward moving the buffalo. Santa would just have to wait. We had absolutely no money for Christmas gifts, which didn't matter anyway. I had received the best gift of all.

The week before Christmas was not exactly an opportune time to arrange to move buffalo, and I needed to make sure that Mike, the buffalo rancher, was still willing to take The Girls into his herd. I wanted The Girls off of Gary's property YESTERDAY. I placed a call to Joe, the hauler, and told him that this time, we could really get the buffalo off the property.

Mike was elated that my ordeal was over. He said, "I am glad it worked out that you own the buffalo." That word did not sound right to me. No one should "own" buffalo. An American Icon should only be wild and free. I was just their Auntie, who would always be there for them.

Mike said he would take The Girls into his herd, and I told him I had called Joe, but I would also call his friend Skip, to see who might be available to move them off the property. Skip was a horseman who frequently owned a few buffalo to work with his cutting horses. Mike had suggested that Skip could call Gary and offer to buy the animals for me after the confrontation with Bill the Slaughterer and the deputies. I was so grateful to Skip that he did try to buy them for me, though Gary declined to sell them because of the "legal issues." Mike also gave me the name of another livestock hauler, who had some experience with buffalo.

I called Jack Arnold and told him the good news and expressed my trepidation about the dangers of moving The Girls. I also confided how difficult it would be to leave Whiskey there. Jack said he sure wished he were younger so he could move them for me. He gave me sage advice about handling them, which was the same as was told to me by buffalo experts. Before hanging up, Jack said, "Now don't you worry about those animals. They are tough. They'll do just fine."

Until The Girls were moved from The Concentration Camp, I could not rest. No one called me back that night or the next day, and I grew more anxious and impatient. Finally, I received a call from a very gruff man who said he was referred by Mike's friend, who no longer was in the business. He offered to do the job, but his curt and harsh demeanor was not conducive to moving buffalo. He came across as a man with no patience and no empathy. His high testosterone level could not even begin to compete, what's more succeed, when challenged with the mindset of two determined buffalo girls. As anxious as I was to move them off Gary's property, I had to find someone else.

Two more days into the holiday passed with no response from Joe or Skip. On Christmas Day, I celebrated by going to see the buffalo darlings. Gary was out of town, so I could avoid a confrontation.

The Girls saw me drive up, Whiskey looked over and started running, and The Girls followed. It was just like the good old days, a family reunion, except it would never be the same without Billy. The Girls were excited and happy to see me and eager to receive their treats. Napini even ate out of my hand and didn't try to charge me. She looked as if she had a resigned acceptance of life without Billy. She seemed sad, and I knew exactly how she felt.

I told Nappy and Minko why I had not been able to see them and all about the lawsuit. I told them how much I loved them, and that they were going to a buffalo ranch on vast acreage where they would live their lives with other buffalo pals. Finally, I asked them to trust me. With everything that had happened, I knew that was asking a lot.

Nappy had never been cooperative with anything, ever, and I doubted she would start now. What's more, cooperation from bison in general doesn't exist. They will go where they want to go, so you have to make them believe it was their idea to go there. You can't try to convince them, cajole them, or even suggest that they do anything they don't feel like doing. Add to that, the confinement involved with moving buffalo makes them claustrophobic. Like I said, they ain't cattle.

After about a week, Joe finally called, and we made a plan for the move. We would open the fence gate, and then Joe would back the trailer tight up against the opening. Then he would open the gate to the trailer and put the food in it, instructing Gary not to feed the animals. If no other food would be available to them, they would have to go in the trailer to eat, and they would become comfortable with it. We would put up a temporary corral surrounding the trailer with a gate so we could confine them and lead them into the trailer. Great plan…. easier said than done with buffalo.

However, with food also being involved, Whiskey and Minko might get in Napini's way, and we did not want them to get hurt. Once Napini would realize she was locked in the corral, she would most certainly start charging anything in sight. I remembered Charlie's accident ramming into a corral, and I feared for Nappy's safety too. There are so many "ifs" and "buts" to worry about with wild animals, and you can only count on the unpredictable. Instead, I chose to count on God. Poor God. I was back again, pleading for more miracles.

I received a call from Skip. He told me that Mike decided he did not want to accept The Girls into his herd unless they had blood tests. Skip said he had the handling facilities, and they would have their vet, Dr. Goss, draw the blood samples. Skip said he would keep The Girls a few days with his buffalo, and if the tests proved they were healthy, they could join Mike's herd. I was surprised that Mike did not call me himself, and disappointed that the move would be more traumatic for The Girls. But I had no other option that would allow a protest.

The next day Skip called again and said Mike really did not want The Girls. My untested blood drained to my feet. Skip said he knew of a buffalo rancher about 90 minutes away who would take them. I knew who Skip meant. Jed Hammon had a small bison herd in Lincoln, Ca. but he sold some of them for meat. Skip assured me that Jed did not slaughter the females, and that my girls would live out their lives on 100 acres roaming free. I was concerned and not convinced about this sudden change of plans. I had not seen the property, the bison, or talked to Jed. But I trusted Mike and after all, Skip had tried to help me before.

Skip sensed my hesitation and said, "If you put the buffalo with Mike, who really doesn't want them, you will rarely get to see them. Jed will let you visit and if they were my animals, I'd want them at Jed's place.

I asked a few questions like, "Who would own them?" (There's that ugly word again, but it was necessary that I ask.)

Skip said I would own them, but Jed would own the offspring. He said Jed would take care of all their needs. I agreed, but on the condition that I get first right to purchase any babies. I wanted to make sure that one of Billy's grandbabies or step kids wouldn't go to the slaughterhouse. Skip called me back and said everything had been arranged. I asked for Jed's number and thanked Skip for his help.

I later learned from Jed, that Skip owed him money for two bison. The bison died, but Skip never paid for them. Therefore to pay off his outstanding debt to Jed, Skip's clever scheme arranged for Jed to own Nappy and Minko. Skip never actually called Jed about the arrangement we discussed, and Mike told me months later that he definitely would have taken The Girls. Billy's innocent girls were used as a ransom and Jed, Mike and I were unknowing participants.

Without any of us knowing all this, I called Jed the following day and thanked him for taking in The Girls. I made sure he would never harm them, and he said I could come visit them whenever I wanted. Jed was a knowledgeable and caring rancher, in spite of his using several of his bison for meat to defray the costs of keeping the herd. I felt that we had finally found a home for The Girls where they would lead as natural of a life as possible. Perhaps someday I could help find a way for Jed to keep his herd intact without having to sacrifice any of them.

Mary informed Gary that Joe, the hauler, and I would be coming to set up the temporary corral and trailer and explained the plan for moving the buffalo. We needed Gary's cooperation, and I knew that would be tough to receive. He agreed to the plan, telling Mary he was headed out of town, and that he had asked his neighbors to look after the bison and Whiskey.

As Joe and I were putting up the temporary corral, we noticed the neighbor throwing hay over the fence. Joe and I said nothing, but we both knew things were not going to go as planned. Gary was not going to cooperate and apparently told his neighbor to feed the animals. If they had food in the pasture, they would not go into the trailer. It would be a dining coach strictly for Whiskey, and he would have no problem going in.

As we set up the corral, Napini stood by and watched our every move, listening to our every word. After sizing everything up, she was unimpressed and turned her back in defiance, walking to the barn. She was letting me know this wasn't going to be easy.

I was instructed to inspect the trailer every day to see if food were missing and if there were any evidence The Girls went in. But for the next three days, it was strictly a dining room for Whiskey.

On New Year's Eve, while I was leaving Billy's Place after inspecting the trailer, the neighbor lady pulled up. She got out of her car, slammed the door and walked toward me in battle mode. She had never acknowledged me in the months she had seen me visit and feed the animals, even after giving her a friendly wave. Now with her feet stomping toward me, I was ready for acknowledgement in the form of a real lip spanking.

I said, "Hello . . ."

And she interrupted, "You aren't supposed to be here. I hope you are happy ruining these people's lives. These animals were fine before you showed up and made them sick. Why don't you go back where you came from and leave us alone?"

I pondered whether these were rhetorical statements and questions, but as I was pondering, more kept coming. Even though I knew she was not interested in having a conversation, I figured I'd stay calm and try to reason with her. If we were to get into a mean-spirited screaming match, I knew I would have no chance against this seasoned pro.

How do you answer someone who has horses and does not know where parasites come from? She obviously had listened to Gary and believed you fed them to an animal. I felt so sad for her horses, since they must surely be plagued with them.

I said, "I would like you to come to my home and sit down with me, and I will show the proof......"

Again, Maximus Interruptus got even louder, "I don't need to see anything!"

I tried my hand at interrupting, "Well, if you refuse to hear my side, then you cannot properly judge anything."

Reasoning with this woman was futile, as her voice became a full-fledged scream," I saw these animals every day for six years, and they were fine." There it was again, the four letter word that was used so obscenely.

I was reminded that she drove by Billy every day and watched him starve to death. That heartlessness made me so angry and I shouted back, "Well, how could you drive by while Billy looked like a skeleton? He only weighed 580 lbs. when he died, and you think he was FINE?!" I was so angry thinking about Billy suffering for so long, but I was disappointed in myself that I fell into the trap that screamers set for you to join them.

She stomped off to her car saying, "Go back to where you came from!"

I never understood the reasoning of people who come from one area to another, and then proclaim, since they were there before you were, you have less status than they do. It's a ridiculous point since there is always someone there before everyone else arrives. The only people who can legitimately claim the "I was here first" trophy are Native Americans, and I don't see that they ever got any respect or special treatment because of it. I guess some people feel we should all be assigned a number, like at the Motor Vehicle Department, to tell us what order in line we should be when we move somewhere else. This screaming neighbor said she "had been here for over 20 years". I responded that I had been here over 11 years, which blew her theory that I was some newbie. I wasn't quite sure if the nine year difference was enough for me to have to give up all claim to being a viable human being, worthy of being accepted in "these here parts."

Then I said something really stupid, "We are all Americans, you know." She screamed a few obscenities, a few of the same ones I had heard from

Gary and his Clan, so I deduced there might be something fouling their neighborhood water supply.

On that fateful day on September 11, 2001, all Americans came together. There was no feeling of you versus us, white or black, rich or poor, country or city people. We were all one. . . Americans. We so soon forget the things that are really important. A national tragedy had to teach us that we are not each other's enemies, and the real enemy is out to destroy us and our way of life. To label each other the enemy, based on geographical differences within our own country, is ludicrous. If we have differences, it doesn't make us despicable. The politicians and the media feed on this division and it has led to such acrimony that our government has become virtually dysfunctional. Shame on us for buying into this. Gary's neighbor had bought it hook line and sinker. The fact that I had reminded her that we are the same was revolting to her and made her even more furious, as she sped up her driveway to get away from me.

And that was my introduction to 2010. Happy New Year!

I called Mary and told her about the neighbor feeding the animals. I asked her to call Gary and insist he not feed them. When she spoke to him, he was furious that the buffalo were still on his property. Mary told him that they would continue to be, if he didn't stop feeding them. In order to move them, they had to go into the trailer. They would only go in the trailor if that were their only food source. Mary and I were amused at the irony of Gary finally deciding to be diligent about feeding the animals when he wasn't supposed to.

After another two days, it appeared that Nappy and Minko had been eating in the trailer, so Mary informed Gary that we would be coming to move them the following day.

Buffalo moving day was cold, rainy, and miserable. The pasture, which had been covered in feces, had now become a stinking cesspool. The non-porous clay in the ground makes accumulated raindrops turn into standing water, and when distributed, becomes almost like thick wet cement combined with equal parts manure. No animal should have to live in this filth, what's more eat off of it.

I even felt sorry for my knee high, black rubber boots, having to sink ankle deep into this stinking muck. If those boots knew where I was taking them, I am sure they would have run off on their own.

Joe, Robert, and I drove up and headed for the corral. The buffalo, being intelligent and curious, came over to see what we were doing. I threw carrots out to them, feeling guilty they were landing on the ground. Minko came up to me, and I fed her by hand. Nappy knew something was up,when she spotted the cowboy stranger, and she was not about to take the bait. She walked a few feet into the corral and then quickly turned and ran out, with Minko in tow.

They stood on the other side of the corral and watched us suspiciously. Gary's Clan, consisting of his sister, brother, mother and I suspected the family friend, Bud Weiser, walked down from the house to give us a piece of their minds. They were calling me all sorts of names I would never answer to and said I was going to "come up missing one day." If you were going to threaten someone's life, it's not very wise to do it in front of a witness. Bud Weiser was no real friend to this family.

Throughout all of the screaming, foul language, and threats, Joe, Robert, and I did not say a word. While Joe's lips stayed closed, his facial expression was clear. It was very unfair to act like this with a perfect stranger who was just there to do his job. Gary's sister was lucid enough to realize this, and she finally said, "Sorry son, I know you are just doing your job." But that didn't stop them and the haranguing soon continued.

I walked back into the pasture with a big carrot in hand, staying next to the corral post in case I needed protection.

I said, "Come on, Nappy girl. We are doing all this for you. You are going to a wonderful place and you'll have a beautiful new guy. Please cooperate, Nappy."

And with that, Napini suddenly bolted full speed toward me. I had asked her to come but not with this much enthusiasm. She was coming head on and I could not see her tail to let me know her intentions. I stepped back to grab the post, in case I needed to jump into the corral if she decided she wanted a piece of me instead of the carrot. As I watched the distance grow slimmer between me and 1000 lbs. of muscle on the run, my boot became swallowed up in the feces-clay-quicksand, and I fell down, on top of my other foot.

Gary's sister had been watching from above on their deck and yelled, "Napini, that's it! She's the devil! Kill her!"

For one split second I felt sheer terror and looked up, directly into Napini's eyes. Then, she did that infamous buffalo turn on a dime, and headed away from me. I grabbed the post to pull myself back up so I could free my boot with my sock still inside. My bare foot was buried deep in the cold sewer mud.

I was no longer afraid. If Napini had wanted to hurt me, she had the perfect opportunity. I had been on the ground, helpless and defenseless. That was when I knew for certain that she and I had bonded after all. Napini had made her own decision. I was not the devil, I was her Auntie . . . the one who had fed her and faithfully taken care of her family, mucked out their stall, delivered fresh water, and spent hour upon delightful hour just being there. Napini had even brought her baby to me. She had no desire or reason to harm me, and after that experience, I felt even closer to her.

But there was still a job to be done. Covered in muck, I walked over to Minko with a carrot and coaxed her into the corral. She walked over gingerly without her mom, and followed me in. Joe was standing by the trailer door, ready to close it when she went in. I tossed more carrots in the trailer and she jumped right in. Joe slammed the door shut, and we had a brief moment of elation, until the frightened little girl started kicking and slamming into the trailer, desperate to get out. She was crying and thrashing and we were worried she would hurt herself. I heard Jack's words in my head, "Don't worry, they are tough. It will be fine." But it wasn't fine. Robert tried to calm her by giving her assuring buffalo grunts and then kind human words. Napini came into the corral and walked up to the trailer, but Minko's cries were not enough to get her to join her baby in the second compartment, and she turned and ran up the hill. Even though Napini had always proven to be self-centered, I was very surprised that she would leave her baby in such distress. Minko continued to cry for her mom's help. It obviously wasn't breaking Napini's heart like it was ours. I quickly called Jed to get his opinion about whether we should bring Minko to the ranch alone or bring them together. We all agreed we should not separate them. The move would be stressful for them as it was and they would do better together. So we let Minko out of the trailer. She stood outside for a few minutes shaking with terror. Then she ran up the hill to join her mom. We felt like the lowest form of child abusers.

After consulting with Jed, we decided to try again in a few days. We realized we would need to get Napini in the trailer first. Jed heard the pain and disappointment in my voice and said, "I'll come out with my Dad and we'll get them loaded." I was so thankful to know that someone with 20 years of experience with bison would come move my girls. Of course, Jed did not know Napini.

We decided to wait a week to let The Girls forget about the experience and to have more time for them to become accustomed to the corral and the trailer. But every day that those girls were still on that property seemed like an eternity. Every day that Gary was still in our lives was pure hell.

One night around midnight, we were entertaining guests, when Robert's cell phone rang. He looked at the caller number and knew it was Gary. He was afraid something might be wrong, so he answered it. The only thing that was wrong was Gary and his best buddy, Bud Weiser, had been partying all night together. Gary's slurred speech told Robert that he wanted him to come over to his house so he could "kick his {*CENSORED*}". When my husband calmly told Gary he did not feel like coming over at midnight to be assaulted, Gary said he was going to kill him and went into an unintelligible tirade of profanity. All this drama was getting old and seemed potentially more dangerous than dealing with the buffalo.

I was careful to schedule the next moving appointment when I knew The Clan would probably not be there, in order to deprive them of practicing more of their four-letter fluency. I also knew what day Gary volunteered at the nonprofit thrift store, so I scheduled the next moving attempt accordingly.

When Jed showed up with three guys, I knew it was going to be a problem. Napini saw four strangers and she wasn't buying anything they had to offer. Jed rearranged the corral, and I went out to the pasture to lure The Girls with carrots. Napini wasn't buying what I had to offer either. In fact, the look in her eyes said she was insulted that I thought she could be fooled so easily, and she kept her distance. I told Jed that she would not come near all these strangers, and they would have to hide in the barn. Buffalo have such keen hearing and she knew they were still there. She stood there sizing up the situation and you could just see the wheels turning in her head. This girl was nobody's fool. After about three hours, she finally did go into the corral, and Jed quickly moved to slam the gate shut. She became a big brown blur, turning around, speeding for the gate, faster than he could close it. Jed jumped out of her way as she barreled past him, but not before she showed him what she thought of his part in the shenanigans by grazing his arm with her horn.

Poor Jed suffered a month with that sore arm. I felt so badly about it. Napini on the other hand, didn't feel the slightest bit guilty. I was afraid Jed would not want to take Napini in after that. But he was a dear one and took it in stride. He felt a lot of empathy for these animals' plight after seeing the place and viewing the sad pictures of when I first met them. He even made excuses for Napini and didn't blame her. And by sticking up for our bratty, head strung girl and genuinely caring, I knew The Girls would be well taken care of at his ranch . . . if we could just get them there.

Jed said the corral needed to be set up differently, and he did not have the equipment, and with his sore arm, I needed to find someone else to move them.

I was beginning to think that the only way to move Napini safely was to tranquilize her. With her intelligence and stubbornness, and with the volatile situation with Gary, we couldn't continue trying, waiting for Napini to decide she'd cooperate. I contacted Dr. Goss, the vet who had been highly recommended by Mike and also by Jack Arnold. Dr. Goss mainly dealt with horses and cattle but he did have some experience with Mike's buffalo. I told Dr. Goss the situation and he agreed to help and come out to assess the situation. He was conscientious, kind, responsive and welcomed advice from bison experts. He was about to find out that his new patients had friends and advisors from all over the US and Canada.

I contacted Dr. Murray Woodbury again in Saskatchewan about tranquilizing Napini and he agreed to confer with Dr. Goss about the risks and complications. I also contacted The Buffalo Guys in Nebraska because I knew they had experience tranquilizing their animals on their ranch. Dr. Woodbury knew how much those animals meant to me, and he strongly advised against tranquilizing them. The safest approach would be to take the time necessary to get Napini into the trailer through behavior modification, just as we had been doing. After researching the sedative with Dr. Woodbury, Dr. Goss did not want to attempt tranquilization because of the danger to his staff. Even one drop of the sedative could kill a human. I trusted Dr. Woodbury completely, and he had again come to my rescue from 1800 miles away. He was nothing short of a buffalo saint.

Dr. Woodbury made me realize that I was allowing Gary to control the operation with his threats and aggression, and I should not allow him to put the animals in jeopardy. I asked Mary to call him again, and explain that we had considered tranquilization to get The Girls moved off his property, but the safest thing to do would be to do what we were doing. She told him that if he wanted the buffalo gone, he needed to be patient and to cooperate. The buffalo would be moved when the buffalo could be moved. No matter how long it took, that is how long it would take. They are wild animals. They ain't cattle.

But who would move them? Joe wouldn't return my call and who could blame him? Who would willingly subject themselves to the wrath of The

Clan? Jed wasn't able to do it. I started calling everyone I could think of and tried not to sound desperate. Everyone referred me to everyone else. Finally someone referred me to a thirty-something cowboy named Jason, who had run the local livestock auction. Jason had experience moving all sorts of animals and even some pretty ornery long horn bulls, but of course, he had no real experience with bison. Jason was described as patient and persistent, and best of all, he had a friendly and open disposition, free from macho interference. When I called Jason and explained the situation he said, " I don't think it will be too much of a problem, when do you want to do it?" Of course, he didn't know Napini.

Thank you Jesus! I told Jason he was a cowboy angel sent from heaven, which made him laugh. He said, "I've been called a lot of things, but an angel is a new one."

On the prearranged day, I met Jason at Billy's place. It was the familiar moving day: cold, rainy, and miserable, with the same conditions on the ground. Jason surveyed the corral set up and said, "We need to change this around. We need two gates and to make the corral bigger." As we began to work, Napini, Minko, and their pal, Whiskey, supervised the operation from a distance.

At one point, I was moving a corral panel, and stepped back into a hole. I lost my balance when my boot got stuck, and I fell flat on my back. I was covered in stench. I quickly started flailing to get back up but it felt like this cesspool was sucking me back down. I looked over at Jason for some help. He was trying desperately not to laugh, but then I started laughing. We both laughed until our sides hurt, and he came to pull me out. Whiskey even came over to see what the fuss was all about. I brushed my smelly gloves across my now darkish brown hair and said, "I can't believe how much I love these animals!" As I walked to my car I yelled to Jason, "In the words of the Governator, I'll be back!"

I was not only filthy. but I was freezing. I put a big garbage bag over my car seat and literally slid in. I took my boots off and left them at the side of the road, since there was no concern that someone would take them. My Jaguar reluctantly drove me home, with the windows rolled down for some decent smelling air and with the heater blasting. Once home, I showered, piled my wet hair up into my black cowboy hat and made sandwiches for Jason and me. Then I drove back to face my pasture opponent for round three.

We gave the buffalo four more days to get used to the bigger corral leading to the trailer. Jason, Robert, and I decided that only the three of us would be there to contain The Girls. Strangers made Napini uneasy which would make the job more difficult, if not impossible. We were trying all angles to make this move successful. Between Jed, Joe, Dr. Woodbury, Jim Matheson from the National Bison Association, three other bison ranchers, Dr. Goss, Jason, Jack, Robert and I, we had a combined IQ of over 2000 trying to figure out the mind of just one smart buffalo girl. It makes you wonder.

When the day came to try the move again, I prayed that this would be the day. Gary had been throwing hissy fits, and we knew his patience was at its end. We all were at wit's end . . . except for Napini.

We had called Jed at his ranch to stand by to receive The Girls when, not if, we got them loaded. For four hours we tried everything we could think of to get Nappy in the corral. She would saunter in just to tease us and then run right back out to torment us. We knew the entire Clan had gathered again because we could hear them laughing. But we were determined that the buffalo would have the last laugh.

Finally, exasperated with our failure, Jason said, "Well, we'd better call it a day and come back again in a few days." My husband and I looked at each other in desperation, and Robert said to Jason, "We don't have any more days, Jason. It has to be today." Jason was just as frustrated, but with his upbeat personality and seeing Robert and I in agony, he said, "Well, okay, let's try something else.

Anyone else but Jason would have thrown in the towel. Jason began thinking about another plan to outsmart Napini. He threw a lot more hay into the corral under the metal cover where the animals usually ate. He told me to stand near the first gate, thinking Nappy would then be comfortable going in with me there. He stood at the second gate, ready to close it when she did go in. He told Robert to stand at the trailer gate, ready to lock her in when she ran into the trailer. Neither of us could see each other, so we would not be able to tell what was happening in front of the other. We stood silent and waited. After about 10 minutes of agonizing silence, Whiskey decided he was ready to eat and entered the corral. Food aggressive Napini couldn't bear to watch Whiskey eat all that fresh fluffy hay in peace when she had none. So she avoided the stranger's gate and came over to my gate to enter the corral, with Minko following right behind. Then the miracle happened: Minko walked past me out of the corral, leaving Napini inside eating the hay.

I said loudly but calmly, "She's in." I closed the gate as fast and hard as I could and began frantically winding baling string around the gate and the post for more strength. I was so afraid Nappy would charge the gate before I had it secured. At the same time, Jason shut his gate. Whiskey and Napini were locked in! I could not see, but I heard Napini's hooves hitting the ground, and then she rammed into the corral. I prayed that she would not hurt Whiskey or herself in her rage and panic. I heard Jack's comforting voice saying, "Don't worry, they'll be fine."

Once The Clan heard me yell that Nappy was closed in, they started screaming, "You'd better not hurt Whiskey!" They were all screaming at once, so most of it just sounded like noise. I motioned for them to be quiet, to not upset Napini any more than she was. Gary's sister then started swiftly walking toward me, threatening to do me bodily harm if I told her what to do again . . . . blah blah blah. Since I couldn't envision myself mud wrestling with her, I turned away and concentrated on securing this raging buffalo. Napini ran to my gate and charged into it, lifting it up, along with a big section of the corral. We held our breaths that it would hold. But this gave Jason enough time to get Whiskey out of the corral through his gate. Then he wound the baling string around the gate and post. We had her! She whipped around and saw that Whiskey had escaped, which made her even more agitated. She ran into Jason's gate, lifting it up with the attached corral panels about three ft. off the ground. We held our breaths again. She could not raise the fencing and get under it at the same time. So she let it go, turned around on a buffalo dime, and headed straight into the trailer. By this time, Jason had moved to the trailer gate to help Robert secure it. He shoved the gate over to Robert and he caught it, but before he could lock it shut, Nappy had turned around and rammed it back open with such a force it tore away from Robert's hands. Then she ran into the corral again, lifting it as high as she could. However the combined weight of these corral panels were not allowing her to lift it high enough for her escape, so she turned around and ran back into the trailer. This time Jason pushed it with all his strength, Robert grabbed it and pulled it shut. It was done! After almost nine months spent wishing for this moment, it was over in an instant.

Then another miracle happened. She did not cry, snort, kick, flail, or even utter a sound. We had been concerned about what she would do, once locked in the trailer, and based on the trauma with Minko. But she was completely quiet and resigned. Robert went over to the trailer window to reassure her.

Jason then turned his attention toward Minko, who was standing close to Whiskey for moral support on the knoll under the oak tree. I asked Jason if he wanted me to get her. He picked up a box full of sweet cob and said, "No, I'll do it." He walked over to her, enticing her with the buffalo candy, and she followed him right into the second trailer compartment. We held our breath again when she was locked in, but since her mom was in the compartment next to her, she didn't seem a bit upset. She was ready for the ride of her life . . . and we were too.

I don't believe Gary and The Clan ever thought we would actually get The Girls off the property. They went ballistic. Gary's face was flaming red as he and Bud Weiser yelled to Robert, "You get off my property or I'll kick your {*CENSORED*} REALLY hard."

Robert and I walked swiftly but calmly to our truck, as we wanted to get off his property much more than he wanted us gone.

Whiskey ran to the fence to see us off. Robert gave Whiskey a nose rub, and we told him we would try to think of a way to come back for him too.

We got into the truck and watched the trailer being pulled down the driveway with the precious cargo. Even with the profanity laced ranting, arms flailing, and unfriendly gestures aimed in our direction, we only heard the joy in our hearts. Nothing could possibly interfere with my promise to a dying buffalo about to be fulfilled.

We followed the trailer down the winding road, and I called Jed to tell him the good news: The Girls were coming home! He was so happy for us. It was about an hour and a half ride to the ranch, and all the way The Girls were quiet and calm. I was chatty and exuberant as the day I had dreamed about and had fought so hard for had finally arrived.

But just as every step of this journey had not been easy, we approached the ranch at dusk. Jed wisely recommended we not release The Girls until morning. Safety was the issue, and we agreed to leave them in the trailer overnight and set them free in the morning.

I barely slept that night, making time go by even slower. I thought about each miracle that had happened over the past nine months, and especially that moving day. No one was hurt, and the stress on The Girls was as minimal as one could hope for with wild animals. My cheeks hurt from smiling so much, and God received BIG loving thank yous. I prayed that Nappy and Minko would be accepted into the herd without incident. The release was the last hurdle to jump.

Coming Home

Today was the day! The ride back to the ranch was filled with just as much excitement and anticipation as the night before. It almost seemed surreal that this day had finally come. However, I couldn't help but feel a twinge of pain that Billy wasn't there too.

When we drove up to the trailer, we jumped out to see how The Girls were doing. Robert peeked in, saw them lying down and said, "Good Morning, girls! How was your night?" They were calm and quiet and quickly got to their feet. Jed made a "whoop and a holler" to call his herd over to the pasture next to the trailer. They knew that call meant he had hay for them, and it was a thrill to see them running and to hear the historic noise of buffalo hooves stomping the ground. The herd gathered around, instinctively knowing something new was about to happen. Then Jason and Jed opened Minko's trailer door. Robert and I were standing to the side about 15 ft. away. She stood in the trailer, not knowing if she should leave the comfort of her accommodations. I said, "Come on, Honey. Come see your pals." She gingerly stepped down and then ran past us about 50 ft., stopping cold when she saw the herd. It was so cute to see her thinking, "These guys look like me, smell like me, who are they?" She looked back at us. Napini's door was opened, and she raced out to join her baby. Just as Minko had done, when she saw the herd she stopped short. Both girls then turned around looking to us for assurance.

I said, "Go on, now. Join your new family." They stayed put. Then a big female broke from the herd and walked up to Napini to introduce herself and to escort her in to the family. She and Minko followed, and were greeted with nudges and licks. It was a bit overwhelming for Napini, and she ran back to stand where she had been. Minko however, loved all the attention and mingled around, but finally left to stand next to her mom. A few minutes later, they both walked slowly back into the herd and they were accepted without incident. All the buffalo were milling around for the next 20 minutes, just as we would do at a family reunion, meeting new relatives.

Jed's breeding male, Brutus, was absolutely magnificent, weighing 2500 lbs. or more and standing at seven ft. high. It was obvious by watching him that this incredible beast knew he was Hollywood gorgeous and that he ruled. He spotted The Girls, but did not approach them.

Roaming buffaloes settle into new home

And so, the end of a captivating saga

BY LIZ KELLAR
Staff Writer

Napini and Minko no longer need to roam.

The buffalo cow and calf whose 10-day walkabout last fall captivated the county and sparked a bitter custody battle, have integrated into their new herd. The pair were moved from Dog Bar Road to a buffalo ranch in Placer County two weeks ago and are settling in nicely.

(Billy's Auntie) who took owner Gary to court for possession of the bison after claiming he was neglecting the animals, took legal possession of the buffalo at the end of December.

But it took a month of wrangling — at times literally — to transport the hefty pair.

"The biggest problem was the logistics of getting them from where they were," said rancher Jed

"I went up and tried to load them myself, but I didn't have the right equipment. They're not like cattle. They definitely have a mind of their own. They're a lot faster and more agile."

Jed was happy to add Napini and Minko to improve the genetic diversity of his herd.

"I mostly concentrate on breeding stock," he said. "I've been raising bison for about 20 years."

Once the pair was corralled, it was happy trails, said handler Jason Dailey.

"It just took a little while for

See BUFFALOES A8

BUFFALOES:
Continued from A1

them to come in," he said. "They were a little skeptical, a little nervous ... But it wasn't too bad. Nobody got hurt."

Napini and Minko arrived in Placer County to a warm reception.

"They had a welcome reception of 50 buffalo pals staring at them,"(Auntie)wrote in an e-mail. "A female from the herd walked over to them, and they walked with her into the herd. They were received with nudges and licks, and everyone came over to size up these new kids on the block ...

"After about an hour, the magnificent male headed over the hill, and the herd followed. Nappy and Minko stood for several minutes staring at us, and then Minko turned to join the herd and Nappy followed, literally walking into the sunset.

"It was the perfect storybook ending to this saga."

Gobbling carrots

It began in October, when the two buffalo escaped from their enclosure on Gary's property near Alta Sierra a few weeks after the cow's mate, Bill, died.

The buffaloes had been missing for a week and a half before wind and rain drove them back to Gary's property Oct. 13.

But during their 10-day escape,(Auntie)went public with allegations Gary possibly caused Bill's death, and vowed to find new homes for Napini and Minko.

Gary , for his part, alleged (Auntie)improperly fed his animals, perhaps causing the male buffalo to die earlier in the fall.

In late October, Nevada County sheriff's deputies were called to Gary's property after (Auntie) showed up to take the buffaloes but was not allowed access by Gary. (Auntie)had a document dated in October and signed by Gary giving her the buffaloes, but Gary said the document was no longer valid.

(Auntie) filed a lawsuit for possession and both parties spent time in mediation before Gary agreed to give the two buffaloes up in late December.

(Auntie) went to visit the buffaloes in their new home Saturday.

"I was so excited to see them, yet a bit apprehensive, since the rancher had warned

Napini looks back at the herd with Minko behind. A few seconds later, they walked away with the other buffaloes at their new digs at a ranch in Placer County.

me that after they joined the herd, they would not come to me or my husband anymore," (Auntie)wrote in the e-mail. "I had prepared myself for letting them go and not having the same bond ...

"Just seeing them happy and with the herd, leading the life they were meant to live, would bring its own happiness."

Despite her previous apprehension, (Auntie) and the rancher went out to the pasture, and she was able to feed the two buffaloes, she said.

"I held out my hand full of carrots and baby Minko walked right up to me, as if I had just seen her yesterday," she wrote. "The rancher and I hung out with the herd for a couple of hours."

To contact Staff Writer Liz Kellar, e-mail lkellar@theunion.com or call (530) 477-4229.

As Napini and Minko look to their Auntie for guidance, Brutus approaches Napini to flirt with and comfort her.

After about an hour, he decided it was time to move on, and he began leading the herd down the hill. I walked along with Napini and Minko but they were hesitant to go much farther and they stayed back, still looking over at their Auntie for reassurance. Then the most amazing thing happened. Brutus sensed Napini's hesitation and fear, and he broke from the herd. He walked toward her to acknowledge and reassure her and then stood about eight ft. away in all his majestic glory and confidence. It was just the flirting and special attention that the pitifully lonely girl had needed. After a few minutes, he turned to join the herd on the move. Nappy and Minko were facing me as the herd was passing behind them.

I said, "Go on, girls. I will always love you and I will always be here, but this is where you belong."

Minko looked back to see the herd. Then she looked over to say good-bye to her Auntie and turned around to join her new buffalo family. Ironically, it was Napini who was the last to go. The buffalo girl that had always seemed not to care very much whether I was there or not was hesitant to leave me. She stood looking at me for another few minutes.

I said, "Go on, Honey. It's okay." and then she slowly turned to join Minko.

I watched them walk over the hill, disappearing into a vast and lush natural land where buffalo could truly roam.

Billy was there watching too.

The Pest

While I had such a feeling of relief and thankfulness that The Girls were settled into a wonderful home, it was also bittersweet to lose the everyday contact with them. Jed had said that once they blended into the herd, they would not come to me anymore. It seemed impossible to believe, and too painful to think they would forget me.

I thought of Nappy and Minko every day and hoped they were happy and adapting to their new life. I kept reminding myself that what was best for them was most important. If it meant I would no longer be a part of their lives but they were thriving, then that was the happy ending. We are told real love is about selflessness, but we aren't told how painful that can be.

I laughed as I told my mom that I now understood how she felt when I went away to college. Robert and I felt like empty nesters, and we talked about the buffalo every night and relived our incredible time with them to relieve our loneliness.

I knew that Minko, with her adorable and open personality, would be readily accepted into the herd. But Napini . . . would she get pushed around and put in her place with that bratty attitude? As much as she was a problem child, I still loved her. Even when she irritated me, ignored me, or charged me at the fence, I thought about everything she had gone through and understood.

I waited two long weeks before I called Jed to find out how they were doing and to ask if I could come visit. I began with what would be my regular salutation to Jed, "How are The Girls?"

Jed said Minko had been accepted from the very beginning and readily moved with and in the herd. But at first, Napini had kept to the outskirts. The herd was teaching her what her place was. After the lessons were sufficiently learned, she was fully integrated into her new buffalo family. Jed commented that she had lost that "wild-eyed" look and had really calmed down. The Girls had established themselves so well that he had a hard time distinguishing them. He said he looked for the two buffalo that had the more desirable, darker brown heads. I asked him why a darker brown head was more desirable and he reluctantly told me that for trophy heads, a darker face brought a higher price. That was hard to hear and even more horrific to imagine.

Then I asked if I could come visit. Jed said one of the worst things I could have imagined, and that I was not prepared to hear, "Minko is too tame. She came up behind me, I didn't see her and she nudged me. It really spooked me and it's dangerous. She has no fear of humans, so I don't want you to come around for a while."

I was devastated and silent. After I picked my heart up off the ground I said, "Jed, I have to respect your wishes. However, Minko only came to Robert and me, never to Gary or strangers. She trusts you because we brought her to you. She is never going to change, unless you are mean to her." I thought to myself, "Minko is just like Billy. She is and will always be, Billy's girl."

I knew Jed would not be mean to that precious little buffalo. He did not have meanness in him. I also knew Minko would not do anything aggressive unless she felt threatened. Jed said that she had come up to him and he didn't have any carrots or hay to give her, so she gave him what Jed described as, The Horn. I wanted to laugh, but I said, "Well, then you deserved it. Why the heck didn't you have a treat for her? I'd be mad at you too."

Jed did not have a relationship with his animals like Roger Brooks or I had. I gave Roger and Charlie's book to Jed so he would understand. But Jed was a rancher, and that is a different kind of relationship. I admired Jed as a conscientious and caring buffalo owner. He did not think of them in the same way I did, but how could he when he had to factor in the economics of owning a small herd? He sold off his calves, separating them from their mothers. He sold off other buffalo adults from time to time, so the whole natural dynamic of a herd family was broken. It made me sad that there was a constant disruption of the family and extended family with animals that are so sensitive to it. I was hoping that I might be able to work with him and perhaps other ranchers of small herds, through my idea of a foundation, to keep his herd intact. If I could develop ways to make buffalo more valuable alive than dead, with certain management practices in place, there would be no need to sell them off or slaughter them.

It was not my place to assert my will or beliefs on Jed. We agreed to disagree on certain points and let it be. I knew Jed would keep his word to let The Girls live out their lives on his ranch, and I was eternally grateful.

He had initially said I could come visit the buffalo whenever I wanted. But Jed didn't realize that "whenever I wanted," meant every weekend to me. But I did not want to be a pest, a burden, or a problem. But now I was faced with not seeing my darlings for a long time . . . a time Jed would decide.

I hung up the phone feeling completely empty. I immediately called Robert to tell him the bad news. I was not going to go see The Girls that weekend, or for a long time. He said, "Oh, no. This can't be happening. Not after everything we have gone through."

We reminded each other that the buffalo were safe and happy, roaming free, and that had been our goal. Through many miracles it had finally come to pass. We tried to comfort each other by reminding ourselves that we should be happy and grateful, and we put on a brave front over the phone.

But when we hung up, we each agonized over the feeling that The Girls would think we abandoned them again. To Nappy and Minko, we were family.

I felt as helpless and as out of control as those many months when I took care of Billy and The Kids, through their escape saga, and the two months I could not see them when they returned. It felt like being in the movie *Ground Hog Day*, where you wake up every morning and the same frustrating scenario is playing over again.

I e-mailed Roger Brooks, one of the few people in the world who could understand how I felt. I told him what Jed had said, and now I was separated from The Girls again. Roger reminded me that Jed did have a point. If Minko were standing right next to Jed, and another buffalo approached and accidentally bumped her into him, he could get hurt. I understood that and knew Jed's concern was legitimate. Roger was trying hard to make a good spin out of it, because I knew he was feeling an all too familiar pain for me.

Ranchers tend to feel that by instilling fear in their animals they can better control them. In my opinion and experience, that is not only erroneous but dangerous. Just as a dog will bite out of fear, a wild animal will kill because of it. Fear of a 200 lb. human will not stop a one ton animal that is irritated or feels threatened. I firmly believe that it is through trust, rather than domination and control, that an animal can be handled effectively. An animal that trusts you, and respects you will have no reason to be aggressive, but will have every reason to protect you. Likewise, an animal that fears you will not trust you and anything can happen. Fear breeds pent up anger and aggression, not respect. With Billy, Napini and Minko, I did not try to tame them, control them, or change them. They did what they wanted to do, and each one told me how far they wanted to go. I never stepped over that boundary and it kept me safe, and it let me into a world that few people have known.

As the weeks passed without further contact with Jed, I reminded myself that I had not seen The Girls for two months before Gary gave them up, and when I did finally see them, our relationship picked right up where we had left it. The buffalo taught me that love doesn't have any limits, nor does it have an end. It is only we who can foolishly stand in its way, preventing love from fulfilling its purpose....to bless us with ultimate, lasting, joy and peace. Just the thought of love can move mountains, as it inspires us to do the most wondrous and brave things that we never imagined we could or would do. No matter how much pain comes along with it, love is more powerful. There is nothing that can compare to the joy of a great love and a pure passion. Anyone who has possessed it is fortunate beyond words, and anyone who has received it will never forget it. No, I knew Minko and Napini would not forget their Auntie.

I prayed God would soften Jed's heart and open his mind to a new experience with buffalo. If any being could touch someone's heart it would be precious Minko, with her soft brown eyes and her shy little way of putting her head down and looking up at you. There was no heart she could not melt. I prayed that prayer every day until I am sure God was tired of it. While I couldn't be a pest to Jed, I just wouldn't give God a break . . . "Soften his heart, open his mind."

After two months, I could not hold back any longer. I called Jed and left a message, "How are The Girls? How is that magnificent Brutus? Can I come out?"

Jed called back and said The Girls were great, and he had six new calves. He told me about Minko breaking from the herd and coming up to him. Only this time, he said it in a different, gentler way. He described how he hand fed her with a real affection in his voice! I smiled thinking about a six foot, tough and rugged rancher being manipulated by a little buffalo girl. Nothing could be more natural. Minko was molding another convert.

Jed said, "Come on out and visit." Those were such sweet words.

God had given my passion back to me, and He had answered my prayer. He probably couldn't stand it anymore . . . all the begging, whining and pleading. Whatever the reason, I thanked Him as many times as I begged Him . . . well, almost.

I arrived at the ranch and could hardly wait to see The Girls, as well as the herd. I had also developed a big crush on Brutus, so seeing him would be a thrill. Poor Nappy, I seemed to fall in love with her men.

Jed laughed when he saw my 25 lb. bag of carrots and an equal amount of apples that had been cut into buffalo-sized bites. He said, "You don't have to do that."

I said," I know, but I just love doing it for them." Jed chuckled and shook his head. I said, "Do you think I am stark raving crazy?"

He smiled and said kindly, "No, just a little eccentric."

I laughed and said, "I can live with that. That is what buffalo love does to you."

Jed mounted his ATV with the wagon on the back, full of the grass hay, sweet cob, apples, and carrots I had brought and sped off to the pasture where the herd was grazing. I trailed behind wearing my traditional buffalo outfit and my pink and green floral boots. There were a lot more snakes to avoid at Nappy and Minko's Place. When I caught up with Jed, the herd had gathered around, but one lone buffalo was standing right next to him. As I approached closer, I saw he was hand feeding baby Minko . . . only she wasn't so baby anymore. Jed had that familiar goofy grin on his face that only buffalo can put there. One of Jed's friends was standing a few feet away. Jed said, "Don't be afraid. She is very gentle." I laughed to myself in pure amazement at God's goodness.

I said, "Minko! Baby Minko! Come see your Auntie!" She turned to me, and without buffalo hesitation, began walking to greet her loving Auntie. She stood in front of me and then looked deep into my eyes. Minko had not forgotten her Auntie. I burst into tears and said, "Oh, Honey. I have missed you so much. I love you so much." She looked up at me and held her head up, just as I had taught her to do to get her carrot. I patted the side of her face, just as I had always done. She stayed next to me as I jabbered to her and filled her in on what life had been like without her.

After a while, Jed walked up to us. He hadn't lost his goofy buffalo grin yet, and he tried to pat Minko on the forehead. She tossed her head away. I didn't want to tell him that she didn't like that. I hoped Jed would find the joy in discovering all of these wonderful things about her on his own.

As I was feeding Minko her treats, I was looking for Napini. I spotted her standing about 40 ft. away watching us. I said, "Nappy girl! Come see your Auntie!" And Nappy started walking toward us. I said, "Hi, Honey. Oh Napini, you look so beautiful!" Jed was right. The sad and the wild-eyed look had been replaced with a softer, relaxed appearance. Here, Napini had been able to be just one of the girls, without all the responsibility of decisions and without the fear and heartache of despair. Napini came within eight ft. of me and stopped. She paced side-to-side and then stopped in the same spot. She wanted so much to come to me, but her wildness would not let her. That was just fine with me, and I tossed her a bunch of treats. We were happy, just the three of us gals, munching on carrots, me jabbering away in utter bliss . . . our little family together again.

After a couple of hours Brutus began to lead the herd to roam over the hill. Minko and her mom turned to join them, with stomachs full of Auntie's treats and the knowledge that she would be there for them always. Minko turned to see me one more time, put her head down and tossed it playfully in the buffalo way. I tearfully watched them walk away from me and into the life they were meant to live.

I miss you Billy.

Epilogue

It is now 2014, and much has happened since Napini and Minko arrived at their new home.

In 2012, Minko had a baby girl. The joy I felt was indescribable. It meant that Billy would live on. Minko did not seem to be very bonded to the baby, as most buffalo moms are. A few months after she was born, Jed found her dead in the pasture. There was no sign of any trauma. It explained why Minko was aloof to that baby. Nature tells its creatures if something is wrong. I was heartbroken and hope and pray that Minko will have another baby.

I was committed after Billy died to build a legacy out of his senseless death and to honor the incredible animal that he was. I founded a buffalo nonprofit for the advocacy for the American Bison called, Buffalo Billy's Bison Brotherhood. I also was determined to change the culture in Nevada County dealing with animal abuse. I became the director of an animal advocacy group, Coalition for Animal Welfare and Support, (CAWS). I felt if the many local rescue groups and individual animal lovers would unite into one strong and committed voice against animal abuse/neglect, we could accomplish great things. The community has come together and there has been a shake up in Nevada County Animal Control. Officer Falls and others are gone, and the current officers are doing their jobs diligently. Unfortunately, they are hindered by limited resources but do have the support of the animal advocacy community.

When Billy died, there had not been an animal cruelty case prosecuted in our county in anyone's memory. The outpouring of support for the District Attorney to prosecute these cases has brought about many subsequent animal abuse charges, trials, and convictions, sending a message that animal cruelty will not be tolerated. Even though Billy did not get the justice he deserved, his brief life has made a difference in the lives of other animals and in the way we treat these crimes today.

I finally met my hero and friend, Dr. Murray Woodbury, last year at a bison conference. I was able to tell him in person how much his help and support had meant to me. Poor guy, I just couldn't stop hugging him. He has graciously agreed to be a part of The Brotherhood, probably so I'd stop hugging him.

Sadly, Mary Polansky-Gravatt and Joan Briody have passed away. However, both of these powerful and wonderful ladies read this book and knew that their kind and generous contribution to Billy's story would live on.

My beloved Jaguar hay wagon also finally expired and was purchased by Harry Mok, a Jaguar convertible enthusiast who is restoring it to its former glory.

I see Napini and Minko as often as I can. They are thriving with their herd family. Minko still comes right up to her Auntie for treats and for conversation, and Napini is calm and content to be near me. When I arrive at the ranch and call to the herd, they all come to me. It is such a thrill. Minko has a boyfriend who is a magnificent son of Brutus, and he is so much like Billy. He enjoys hearing me jabber and to be hand fed. He loves having an Auntie too.

In spite of offers from several people to purchase Whiskey, he still remains on Gary's property.

PS:

At press time, Minko had just delivered a new buffalo baby!

Visit the website www.buffalobillysbisonbrotherhood.org

for baby pictures and updates.

Billy Lives On . . .

Buffalo Billy's Bison Brotherhood

Mission Statement:

Buffalo Billy's Bison Brotherhood's
mission is to protect and advocate for the American Bison through
education, promotion, purchase, management, and rescue.

www. buffalobillysbisonbrotherhood.org

Join the Brotherhood for a donation of $35 or more and
receive a great looking T-shirt along with the knowledge
that you are supporting and securing the future
and well-being of the American Bison.

Contact Billy's Auntie: 925-766-1821
or myloveaffairwithbuffalobilly@aol.com
www.buffalobillysbisonbrotherhood.org

Thank you for reading Billy's Book. Please pass it along
to friends or give one as a gift. The proceeds of this book
will go to The Brotherhood to accomplish the goals
outlined in the mission statement.
Billy would appreciate
your support of the Brotherhood.